MW01174672

Bible studies on

Ruth

L. Charles Jackson

Reformed Fellowship, Inc.
3500 Danube Dr. SW
Grandville MI 49418

Reformed Fellowship, Inc. is dedicated to the exposition and defense of the Reformed faith as expressed in the Belgic Confession, the Heidelberg Catechism, the Canons of Dort, and the Westminster Confession and Catechisms.

Book design by Jeff Steenholdt

Send requests for permission to quote from this book to:
Reformed Fellowship, Inc.
3500 Danube Dr. SW
Grandville MI 49418
Phone: (616) 532-8510
Web: *www.reformedfellowship.net*
Email: *office@reformedfellowship.net*

ISBN-13: 978-1-935369-06-6

To Connie

Contents

Ruth: An Introduction

For centuries the book of Ruth has held a prominent place as one of the Bible's greatest love stories. Ruth has an attractive, "happily-ever-after" quality, where a widow's fortunes turn on a dime from death to resurrection. The story places Ruth in the arms of a powerful man who rescues her from poverty and restores the fortunes of her family. In fact, some people enjoy reading Ruth almost entirely for its romantic qualities. After all, what short story could beat the stunning combination of death and widowhood that concludes with a happy marriage and the birth of a beautiful baby boy!

When Benjamin Franklin was a diplomat to the French courts, he was reputed to have read the book of Ruth in a meeting of the French king and French nobles. They were impressed with what they exclaimed to be one of the most profoundly beautiful love stories that they had ever heard. If this is true, Franklin was not alone in his assessment that Ruth was an amazing short story. One theologian says, "It is a tale of charm and delight," and another hails it as "the loveliest complete work on a small scale, handed down to us as an ethical treatise and idyll." Another scholar asserts that "no poet in the world has written a more beautiful short story."[1]

The book of Ruth is named for one of the principal characters of the story. Neither Ruth nor the two other

---

1   David Atkinson, *The Message of Ruth: The Wings of Refuge* (Leicester: InterVarsity, 1983), 25.

main characters, Naomi and Boaz, dazzle us with any of
the mythical qualities so common to the heroes or the
heroines of classical antiquity. For instance, none of the
cast of players would leap onto the pages of *Plutarch's
Lives* or demand a place in one of Homer's epic poems,
and Boaz is certainly not Beowulf. In fact, we do not have
a single record of the main characters accomplishing any
extraordinary feats in war or politics. They seem to be
ordinary people dealing with the ordinary problems of life,
but with a steady faithfulness to God. This might be one
of the qualities so striking in the story of Ruth, especially
when one combines it with the attractive features of a
beautiful young woman discovering love after the death of
her husband.

While the story of Ruth is filled with a moving portrait
of love and emotion, it is more than a quaint little tale of
deep sorrow and passionate love, and this is where the story
becomes the most genuinely satisfying. Ruth is actually
a work of redemptive history. When you read Ruth with
attention to its theological qualities, you pleasantly discover
that Ruth contains much more than a beautiful love story
about how a boy meets a girl. Indeed, when theology guides
you through the story of Ruth, it doesn't dampen its quality
as a love story like an overly professorial preacher. On the
contrary, you are dazzled with a miraculous combination
of human love flawlessly and providentially guided by the
sovereign and artistic hand of divine love. Human romance
becomes a guide to the more stunning qualities of heavenly
love that fills the brief pages of this amazing little story.
This is especially the case when those of us who live in
faithfulness to God discover that Ruth's story is also our
story; it is the story of the gospel.

Date of Writing
The book of Ruth does not provide any direct identification

about when it was written in the story itself. The narrative opens during the end of the period of the judges ("when the judges judged" [1:1]). The opening lines point to a probable date for the book during the early monarchy of Israel (c. 1000 BC). In most English versions of the Bible, Ruth follows the book of Judges. This arrangement, though not consistent with its sequence in the Hebrew canon, accords well with the chronology of the story itself.

The earliest date that Ruth might have been written was probably when David was anointed king (1 Sam. 16). It was certainly not written after David's reign, especially since the genealogy at the end of the book of Ruth is only three generations before David. The genealogy indicates that the latest date for Ruth was probably during the pinnacle of David's fame, since a later date would more than likely have required the inclusion of Solomon's name in the genealogy. It is hard to imagine that the author would have written during or after Solomon's reign without mentioning this great king's place in the genealogy.

Author

Some have argued that the prophet Nathan wrote Ruth. It is more likely, however, that the author was Samuel, who also wrote the book of Judges. The book itself does not disclose its author, but Hebrew tradition from the earliest of times ascribes the book to Samuel, and there is no reason, either in the text or from external sources, to question this tradition. The brevity of the genealogy in 4:18–22 also supports an earlier date of composition, which would align nicely with Samuel.

Samuel had good reason to write such a book. He knew that his anointing of David (1 Sam. 16) had the potential to cause division between the northern and southern tribes of the nation (2 Sam. 1–5). Thus, he was happy to demonstrate that David was from the line of Judah, fulfilling Jacob's prophecy (Ruth 4:12, 18; cf. Gen. 38; 49:8–12).

Old Testament Stories and Our Interpretative Approach
Because of his rich mercy towards men, God has given us the gospel message in beautiful stories. In fact, the bulk of biblical literature is in narrative form. These Old Testament stories contain images of the grace of the Lord Jesus Christ on every page. What we discover when reading the story is not merely a love story or a series of moral lessons; we find the message of redemption; we come face to face with the gospel in this story.

The text is a narrative of Ruth's actual experience as well as a story filled with theology; it is *theological narrative.* Jesus outlines this approach to the Old Testament as he speaks to the disciples on the road to Emmaus: "And beginning at Moses and all the Prophets, He expounded to them in all the Scriptures the things concerning Himself" (Luke 24:27).

This means that, although we must handle the text of Scripture according to its literal, historical, and grammatical meaning, we are not allowed to neglect the redemptive or Christ-centered purpose of the text. In other words, a literal approach is not in conflict with a redemptive-historical approach to the text; they must go hand-in-hand.

By *redemptive-historical* we mean the connections the story has not only immediately to the people in Ruth's day but also to salvation history and to the story of the gospel as it relates to Jesus. This means that Ruth's story is our story, because we hear a fresh, beautiful account of the gospel and God's love for sinners that is connected to the coming of Jesus our Savior.

This is true of Old Testament stories in general. Jonah, for instance, was a literal man who actually and historically experienced the events that are described in his prophecy.

The book of Jonah is not a parable or a work of fiction. It is not an allegorical or mythical illustration of theological truths. It is an actual, historical, and prophetic narrative; it is a theological/redemptive story.

Covenant Theology

Ruth's story fits into and is connected to the unfolding of God's covenant of grace in Jesus Christ. As Meredith Kline notes about the Old Testament, "A literary dimension is added to the functional in our identification of the Old Testament in all its parts as a covenantal corpus. Our thesis is then that whatever the individual names of the several major literary genres of the Old Testament, as adopted in the Old Testament their common surname is Covenant."[2]

What a beautiful gospel story, displaying God as holy and sovereign as well as tender and compassionate toward needy sinners of all tribes and all nations!

This gospel message is unmistakably clear in the story of Ruth. In remarkable and vivid images, God tells us one of sweetest and most touching stories of all time. No matter who you are or what you think about yourself, if you submit to God, you will be blessed. If, however, you do anything else, you will be damned, and you will deserve it. This message bursts the bounds of any man-made theology. This story unfolds before us in all the vivid colors of browned fields burned into a famine-riddled countryside. A sensitive reader can feel the faith dilemma of Naomi and Ruth not in the pounding of a pulpit, but in the heart-pounding and gut-wrenching loss of fathers, sons, and husbands, combined with the torturous humiliation of returning to a land of certain ridicule and painful memories of days gone by. Yes, this is the gospel in a story that we will not soon forget.

---

2   Meredith G. Kline, *The Structure of Biblical Authority* (Eugene, OR: Wipf & Stock, 1989, 1997), 47.

Old Testament narrative is not randomly pulled from
the memory of ancient Jews because they make for good
bedtime stories for little Jewish children. The stories in
the Old Testament are a record of redemption that God
has sovereignly structured to contain a twofold yet unified
purpose, telling us about a specific historical story while
also teaching us about our own story in Christ. The story
does not contain a "different or higher sense, but a different
or high application of the same sense."[3] We can experience
this for ourselves as we study the story of Ruth. Just like
the disciples on the road to Emmaus, we can feel our hearts
burn within us as we encounter our own story in the story
of Ruth.

Typology as a Key
When we read the Old Testament, we need to appreciate
what theologians call *typology*. The Old Testament is not
a collection of fascinating moral stories; it is the story
of redemption that in a variety of amazing literary and
artistic ways teaches about Jesus. What do we mean by
the word *typology?* For a helpful look at this subject see
R. T. France's book, *Jesus and the Old Testament: His
Application of Old Testament Passages to Himself and His
Mission.* France helps us to read Old Testament books with
an appreciation for what theologians call typology: "The
word *typology* comes from the Greek word, *tupos,* which
means a pattern or model. Typology will, therefore, be
concerned with persons, events, etc., which are viewed as
models or patterns for other persons, events, etc."[4]

---

3   See Patrick Fairbairn, *Typology of Scripture,* 2 volumes in 1
    (Grand Rapids, MI: originally published in 1900, Kregel Publications,
    1989), 3.

4   R. T. France, *Jesus and the Old Testament: His Application of Old
    Testament Passages to Himself and His Mission* (Downers Grove, IL:
    Intervarsity, 1971), 39.

This is not the same as allegory, which says that a person, place, or event within a story does not stand on its own but exists merely to represent something else. An allegorical reading associates the story with mere symbolism. A type is an event that stands on its own, but as an event it also points forward to the coming of another event for which it provides a pattern.

Typology is grounded not in mere images but in actual history that contains theology. So we maintain that Jonah was an actual, historical man who truly and literally was swallowed by a giant fish that God had preordained for that purpose. The whole story was a real event of history, but one that God had sovereignly arranged and artistically designed to act as a pattern of his work in the future. This is *theological history* or *redemptive narrative*.

This approach is stunning when you grasp that God did not merely create a story, as an ingenious human author would do by using his imagination, but he brought the story to life in time and in space for his glory and for our salvation. While the best human authors craft stories that are pure fiction, God creates actual, historical stories, which become better than any story ever imagined in the minds of the world's most creative authors.

It is even more amazing when we consider that we are reading a story that is part of a larger narrative that God is artistically and sovereignly creating in history. In the Bible there is an overall narrative, or what we might call a *metanarrative*. This is the overarching story of redemption that is unfolding as it leads us directly to Jesus. So Richard Gaffin notes, "Only gradually has orthodox scholarship come to recognize that biblical revelation is given as an organically unfolding process, that is, as a history, and that dealing with the biblical writers in terms of their respective places in this history, that is with respect to their individual contributions, is not only desirable but necessary."⁵

This is precisely how we must approach the book of Ruth, as part of the organic unfolding of God's history of redemption, as Sinclair Ferguson explains, "The book of Ruth is part of the biblical narrative of redemptive history. It describes one more stage in the purposes of God as they moved inexorably towards the final redemption of his people through Jesus Christ."⁶ The Old Testament stories are all part of the unfolding story of redemption, and we should read them with this kind of theological and literary sensitivity. If we do, France shows that we will discover a wealth of meaning:

> There is a consistency in God's dealings with men. Thus, his acts in the Old Testament will present a pattern which can be seen to be repeated in the New Testament events; these may therefore be interpreted by reference to the pattern displayed in the Old Testament. New Testament typology is thus essentially the tracing of the constant principles of God's working in history, revealing a "recurring rhythm in past history which is taken up more fully and perfectly in the Gospel events.⁷

If we may call this a "method," then Jesus taught this method in Luke 24, when he explained that the entire Old Testament should be approached with eyes open to see the covenant of grace and his redemptive work as the focus. The narrative is filled with redemptive images that teach us of Christ and the covenant of grace.

5   Richard B. Gaffin, Jr., *Resurrection and Redemption: A Study in Paul's Soteriology* (Phillipsburg, NJ: P & R Publications, 1987).

6   Sinclair B. Ferguson, *Faithful God: An Exposition of the Book of Ruth* (Wales: Bryntirion Press, 2005), 13.

7   France, *Jesus and the Old Testament*, 39.

Our Story

Thus, when we read and when we study the book of Ruth not merely as a love story or a moral lesson but also as theological narrative, we find that Ruth's story is also our story. The gospel of life is taught in the story of Ruth. As such, our story is hidden in her story. Like Ruth, we were dead and without hope, were it not for the coming into our lives of our faithful kinsman-redeemer. We, like Ruth, long for bread in the midst of famine and pain; Christ provides us with nourishment. We long to go to the house of bread to find such food. We, too, long for King Jesus to reign complete in our own lives and in those around us. We know he is the legitimate ruler who saves his people. We also hope, as Ruth hoped, that God looks kindly towards those who respond to him with faith, and so we fall down as Ruth fell down, and we cling tightly to the hope of Messiah. So much is here in this story that is also our story. Some of you may be able to relate intimately to the themes of helplessness, widowhood, and hunger. But all of us can relate to the timeless themes of redemption, because they are universal to man's great need of God.

When you read the book of Ruth with Christ as its center, I hope you will experience the same thing the disciples did on the road to Emmaus. They heard the Old Testament expounded, and they responded, "Did not our hearts burn within us while He talked with us on the road, and while He opened the Scriptures to us?" (Luke 24:32).

Questions for Consideration

1. What are some of the initial reasons that Ruth is such an appealing story?
2. Who are the three main characters in the story of Ruth?
3. How does the author describe the main characters?

4. What guides the reader through the story of Ruth?
5. What is the most likely date for the book of Ruth?
   Why?
6. Who wrote the story of Ruth?
7. The Bible is written in what form or genre of literature?
8. Why is Luke 24:27 important for our understanding of
   the book of Ruth?
9. What role does covenant theology play?
10. What is typology?
11. What is allegory?
12. How is Ruth's story our story?

Ruth as Literature

God knows the power of a great story, and the book of Ruth is a great story. Great works of literature are often more capable of inspiring souls than all of the scholarly arguments that could fill a library. This is true of Ruth's story as a great work of literature. Leland Ryken says, "There is a quiet revolution going on in the study of the Bible. At its center is a growing awareness that the Bible is a work of literature and that the methods of literary scholarship are a necessary part of any complete study of the Bible."[1]

When reading Ruth or any other book of the Bible as literature, we should use literary analysis to study the structure, the style, and the content of the book. Robert Alter, a world-renowned expert in biblical literature, notes,

> By literary analysis I mean the manifold varieties of minutely discriminating attention to the artful use of language, to the shifting play of ideas, conventions, tone, sound, imagery, syntax, narrative view point, compositional units, and much else; the kind of disciplined attention, in other words, which through a whole spectrum of critical approaches has illuminated, for example the poetry of Dante, the plays of Shakespeare, the novels of Tolstoy . . . The Bible's value as a religious document is intimately and inseparably related to

---

1 Leland Ryken, *How to Read the Bible as Literature* (Grand Rapids: Zondervan, 1984), 11.

its value as literature.[2]

At this point some may say, "Yes but the Bible is not like Shakespeare or Dante; it is the authoritative Word of God." However, Alter argues that this sort of critical analysis of the Bible's literary art and structure, "far from neglecting the Bible's religious character, focuses attention on it in a more nuanced way."[3] To treat the Bible as a work of literature does not require us to treat it as if it were exactly the same as all other literature.

A literary approach limits us to the meaning of the author's actual words, and it liberates us to investigate the use of images as part of the literary structure of the book with more sensitivity to God's literary, artistic beauty. This enables us to read with more sensitivity to the theological instruction that comes by way of divine artistry. When we pay careful attention to the literary qualities of the whole Bible, it strengthens rather than weakens the theology of the story.

We are free to enjoy God's artistic work as he uses the art of language to communicate to us beautifully. One author says,

> Where the visual artist works with paint, clay, and bronze, and as a craftsman penetrates deeply into the secrets of his materials, the writer uses language. It is a good starting point for us as readers to realize that whatever a text does, it does through language . . . Good readers will, in a way, follow in the writer's footsteps by loving language and

---

2 Robert Alter, *The Art of Biblical Narrative* (New York: Basic Books, 1981), 12 & 19. Please note that Dr. Alter is not a Christian, and his analysis *per se* would not lend itself to a Christ-centered interpretation. However, his emphasis on the literary and artistic qualities of the Bible is a great aid in overall biblical studies. See also the Israeli Bible scholar, Shimon Bar-Erfrat's work, *The Art of the Biblical Story* (Tel Aviv: [s.n.], 1979).

3 Alter, *Biblical Narrative*, 12.

handling it creatively.[4]

Jesus is truly an artistic redeemer! We can be amazed when we see the connection between God's sovereign work in the past and his present work in our own lives. Imagine this: God was thinking about you and me when he crafted the story of Ruth and Boaz thousands of years ago! This brings new life to Paul's statement that we are God's workmanship in Christ Jesus (Eph. 2:10). Paul uses the word *poema*, translated *workmanship* in this passage. Like Ruth and Boaz, we are the poetry of God.

When we read the Bible as literature, we must ask relevant literary and theological questions about the images that Old Testament stories use. We should ask, "Is this a common image in the Bible?" "Is this image used anywhere else in a similar context?" "How is this word or phrase used in other parts of the Bible, and is there a connection?" "What has gone before this particular item, and in what way is it connected to the future?" These and many other questions help to guide us into fruitful avenues of study when it comes to Old Testament stories.

At this point some conservative interpreters begin to get nervous. They may conjure up images of medieval scholars who used allegorical interpretations to hash out all kinds of fanciful stories for preaching. Worse yet, some of them immediately jump to the conclusion that using literary techniques also requires us to adopt liberal theological assumptions. Again, I will note that a redemptive or covenantal approach to the text prohibits fanciful or whimsical interpretations, because we are anchored to the meaning of the story as a work of literature. Likewise, it does not necessarily undermine the basic authenticity and authority of the Scriptures. The text describes historical

---

4   J. P. Fokkelman, *Reading Biblical Narrative: An Introductory Guide* (Louisville, KY: Westminster John Knox, 1999), 28.

events that actually took place. We are limited, therefore, to the literal meaning of the text, and we are bound to use logical methods of interpreting Scripture with Scripture. This does not undermine the authority or authenticity of the Bible as the Word of God.

Respecting the Bible's literary qualities guards us from trying to transform the beautiful poems and stories in Scripture into abstract theological propositions. Leland Ryken helps us here:

> If we read the Bible as literature, we must be active in recreating the experiences and sensations and events it portrays. We must be sensitive to the physical and experiential qualities of a passage and avoid reducing every passage in the Bible to a set of abstract theological themes. If we have "antennae" only for theological concepts or historical facts, we will miss much of what the Bible communicates, and will distort the kind of book it is.[5]

This is a wonderfully liberating approach to the Bible. We are not loosed into a realm of allegory, nor are we compelled to agree with the theological assumptions of the higher critical schools of thought, which treat the Bible as if it were not the authoritative Word of God. Rather, we are liberated to use our image-making and image-perceiving capacities as image-bearers of God. We are also free to probe into the various theological connections that we expect to find in our story to the redemptive metanarrative or, in laymen's terms, to the story of salvation in history. In Ruth, for instance, if we had nothing else but the genealogy at the end of the story, we could see that Ruth's story is intimately connected to the coming of Jesus, and thus to our story.

Ruth's conclusion, written about 1,000 BC, telescopes us forward to the beginning of Matthew 1, which (not

---

5   Ryken, *The Bible as Literature*, 20–21.

randomly) begins with the same royal genealogy. We are required to ask the appropriate literary questions, which link us to the necessary theological/covenantal questions, such as "How does this story fit into the whole story of redemption?" For example, does Ruth's story help us as we read to understand our own story in Christ? If so, what are the connections?

The book of Ruth is a highly structured narrative that definitely points us to redemptive themes. For instance, there are words and phrases that are repeated using a kind of parallelism. In certain places the text is so highly structured that some scholars have suggested Ruth was originally a poem that was transformed into a popular narrative.[6] Thus, in particular areas there is an underlying poetic structure that highlights specific themes. Indeed, we don't need to search too carefully to see this kind of structure.

Resurrection through the Faithful Husband/Kinsman-Redeemer

If it were possible to summarize the theme of Ruth, we could say that Ruth is a story of resurrection through a faithful husband. The historical context of Ruth reinforces this theme. For example, once the people of God had received Saul as the king they so desperately wanted (in spite of the warnings that God had given them in Judges), they found that he was not a true husband to Israel. He was not a faithful husband for the people.

Saul had become a false husband, and the land was in need of a true husband. Saul led his family away from the Lord and the promises of the commandments. His kingdom had become unpleasant because he was not a faithful

---

6   See Arthur E. Cundall & Leon Morris, *Judges & Ruth: An Introduction and Commentary* (Downers Grove, IL: Inter-Varsity, 1968), 242.

husband. This false husband led his wife into the ways of the nations and away from the way of the Lord.

Such a setting helps us to appreciate what is happening when Samuel writes that Elimelech was leading his family away from the way of the Lord. Elimelech, a false husband, led his family away from the land where the Lord had commanded the people to stay, and thus led his family away from the Lord. He led his family away from the safety of the Lord, and the result was that he and his family were cursed, and they died. Thus, he left his wife a widow.

Resurrection of the Tribe of Judah

In spite of Elimelech's unfaithfulness, God provides a man who is a model husband from the tribe of Judah. This royal tribe provides a faithful husband who leads the people in the way of the Lord. This husband, in ironic contrast to Elimelech, establishes a godly house with a model husband/king. The highlighted contrast between a faithful and unfaithful husband would have had intense thematic significance to the people of Israel, given the context of recent civil war, and it would have demonstrated clearly the contrast between Saul and David.

David as King

Ruth's story offers a beautiful and powerful argument for the authenticity of David as king of Israel. Yes, God knows the power of a good story, and he uses the compelling images from this sweet story to convince his people of the validity of David as king. We can recall that Saul was still ruling as king when God came to Samuel and told him to anoint David as king. This story prepares the people to acknowledge that anointing.

As you can imagine, Samuel approached this task with great trepidation. Samuel was in mortal danger because Saul was on the throne and was the de facto king.

Nevertheless, Samuel anointed David as the legal heir of the throne. This presents a formidable problem: David is anointed but is not yet on the throne. How would the people become convinced that God was the one who had chosen David? The book of Ruth offers a compelling apologetic for the legitimacy of David as the God-appointed and proper king. When you read this story, you can't reach any other conclusion but that a sovereign, compassionate God has raised up this woman Ruth and this man Boaz at just the right time in just the right way. The sovereign hand of Providence is unmistakable.

Irony
Probably the most powerful literary tool that Samuel uses in the story of Ruth is irony. Irony is when something that usually means one thing is deliberately twisted or changed to point us toward the opposite. It creates a serious incongruity between the expected results and the actual results. Or, as occurs in Ruth, it creates a painful gap between what the characters of the story expect and what the readers of the story expect. Samuel does this not just once or twice as he layers the whole story with irony.

There is a series of ironic reversals in the very opening of the story. The city of bread,[7] or the city of life, becomes a place of famine and death. From there the family leaves to Moab, historically a city of death for Jews. In the face of death, they leave for life and instead receive death. Then, in the face of death, they return again to the city that was once dead but which now is the source of life. In the end they find life in a city that in the beginning was dead.

From the land of death they leave in order to return to the city of bread, Bethlehem. Ruth 1:1–7 comes full circle. This is the theme of resurrection, whereby God reverses the

---

7 Bethlehem means "house of bread" in Hebrew. See below for a full explanation.

plight of his people. Only a few verses into this little story, Naomi comes back full circle to where her story began, in Bethlehem. The author also uses repetition of the word *return* to guide us to the theme of reversal and resurrection. If we are sensitive readers, we can peel back the layers of irony to deepen our appreciation of God's grace and mercy to the needy.

Judah and Bethlehem

Irony is used in the names as well as places we read in the story. For instance, the tribe of Judah and the town of Bethlehem are given standing in Ruth's story. First, we should recall that the tribe of Judah had lost their legitimate standing as heirs in the Promised Land because of the traumatic, incestuous affair that occurred in Genesis 38. You should bear in mind the story of Judah promising his sons to his widowed daughter-in-law Tamar in order to fulfill the levirate laws.[8] However, as Judah denied Tamar her rights under the levirate laws, she tricked him into having an unwittingly incestuous affair that produced his sons, Perez and Zerah. This enormous scandal caused the line of Judah to become illegitimate. Judah's two sons were illegitimate, which disqualified them for acceptance in the assembly of the people of God. "One of illegitimate birth shall not enter the assembly of the LORD; even to the tenth generation none of his descendants shall enter the assembly of the LORD" (Deut. 23:2).

The people of Israel knew that illegitimate children could not be proper heirs of the covenant until the tenth generation. Thus, it is no coincidence that at the end of the book of Ruth we have a listing of generations, a genealogy. Here we see that the genealogy in the last verses of Ruth establishes that David is the tenth generation of the tribe of

---

8   See below and see chapter 10 for a full discussion of levirate law.

Judah from Judah's sins in Genesis 38. The book of Ruth chronicles the restoration of the tribe of Judah and narrates for us how God made David the legitimate ruler from the tribe of Judah, and it points the people of God forward in the hope that the dynasty of David would rule forever.

The story of Ruth reveals how God restored and/or resurrected the line of Judah, thus clearing up potential misunderstanding in regard to David's rule. When Saul was ruling, David's line was potentially hampered by Judah's sin of incest. The whole story of Ruth acts as an excellent apologetic for the legitimacy of David's rule.

The Levirate Law
Ruth offers the reader a rare narrative description of the levirate laws in practice. Her story connects us back to portions of Scripture that help us to unfold the purpose and meaning of the levirate laws. This splendid little tale vividly portrays for us the idea of marriage and inheritance as it relates to the themes God had designed as part of the enigmatic levirate laws.

The levirate laws tell us that if a firstborn son married a woman but died before having a male heir, then one of his younger brothers would have to take the widow as his wife. The firstborn son of this union would then continue the line of the deceased father. Hence, the name and inheritance of the man would not die. Do you see the resurrection theme?

For example, if Bob married Susie, and Bob died before having children, then his brother would marry Susie and produce children. If children were born, the firstborn would be considered Bob's son. This is exactly the principle Onan violated in the story of Tamar and Onan in Genesis 38. Too many people focus on the violation of the idea of birth control from that passage. However, as we learn from the story of Ruth and the purpose of the levirate law, the infraction ran much deeper than Onan's desire for birth control. Onan was a selfish husband who flagrantly disregarded the purpose of the levirate laws and who would rather see his dead brother's name die than to risk his own holdings, bringing a curse on Judah. Ruth's story explains to us how God lifted this curse. Boaz and Ruth keep the law, and the curse is reversed and removed. This brings life to the dead house of Judah and thus provides the way for David to become the legitimate king. To say that Ruth's story is an artistic portrait of the levirate laws in action barely does justice to the mastery of God as the divine artist.

Bethlehem

The theme of resurrection and reversal is scattered throughout the whole story of Ruth and even applies to the town of Bethlehem. Up to this point in history, Bethlehem was considered a rough and somewhat cursed town. Ruth's story reverses this blight and brings the cursed little town of Bethlehem into the spotlight as the birthplace of the house of David, the ruler anointed by God. Today we know that Bethlehem means "house of bread" and that it was Jesus' birthplace. Yet in its earliest days it was not blessed but cursed.

In a variety of ways Bethlehem is used as an important backdrop to the story of redemption. For example, as the story opens, the town is referred to as Bethlehem—house of bread—but ironically the town has no bread. This points us to the covenant curse that applies as the story opens. However, as the Lord is honored, the town is restored to its position as a place of plenty. What happens to Bethlehem can be understood to represent in some ways what happens to the whole world in reference to the arrival of God's blessings or curses. Can you imagine a Christmas season passing without a song that bore reference to the city of Bethlehem?

Faithfulness vs. Faithlessness

There is a strong ironic contrast between faithfulness and faithlessness in the book of Ruth. Elimelech was a faithless husband who sought blessings outside of the covenant. Elimelech's name means "God is king." How could someone with this name reject the covenant and leave the land? Ruth, on the other hand, who is a heathen outsider to the covenant, sought blessings in the covenant and in the land. Where Elimelech had rejected the covenant and left the land of promise, Ruth accepted the covenant and sought to be faithful in the land of the Lord. She becomes faithful in the face of his unfaithfulness. This is highly ironic, since Ruth is from Moab.

Her son was named Obed, which means "slave." Elimelech, whose name means "God is the king," is set in stark contrast to his descendant from Ruth, whose name means "slave." Elimelech, whose name ironically points to the fact that he should have been a slave of God, did not serve God. Obed, whose name means slave (Obadiah, for instance, means "slave of Yahweh"), was actually the child of the levirate marriage, which produced the true king of Israel.

Humble Women and God's Love of the Needy

The book of Ruth is the Old Testament equivalent to the New Testament story of the Good Samaritan. Ruth is one of only a handful of women who are mentioned in biblical genealogies. One of the other women included in those same genealogies is just as theologically important, because she is called Rahab the harlot, and she is intimately connected to the story of Ruth—she is, after all, the mother of Boaz. Like Rahab the harlot, Ruth is given a virtual title, Ruth "the Moabitess." Moab was associated with famine and curses. When Jesus chose to teach the proud Israelites of his salvation, he used the most despised ethnic group of the day, the Samaritans. Likewise, in Ruth God brings salvation from the most unlikely of places: Ruth the Moabitess.

Ruth is ironically a cursed foreigner. Yet in God's great mercy he reverses her condition, and he not only makes her a legitimate member of the covenant community but he also exalts her as the mother of salvation. What a great story! From where does salvation come? Does it come from the proud palaces of Israel? Does God bring a king from the mansions of the city of Jerusalem? No, God brings salvation from humble origins in the womb of a humble woman. What a theme!

Life and Death
Ruth tells a story of two ways: one is a way of life in the covenant, and the other is a way of death outside the covenant. Two ways are set before us in vivid contrast. What better way to teach about the contrast between life and death than in a story like this one!

God as Faithful Husband/Redeemer
The book of Ruth provides an excellent story of the love of a "true husband." There is a stark contrast between the faithlessness of the story's first husband, Elimelech, and the faithfulness and strength of the true husband, Boaz. Boaz comes to Ruth's aid as a selfless servant. He offers himself to her in order to restore her and her seed. When a man becomes the kinsman-redeemer as Boaz became for Ruth, he gives up claims to the firstborn son. This firstborn son belongs to his kinsman. The true husband is faithful, sacrificial, and loving. He lays down his life for his bride and leads her in the way of life. What a profoundly beautiful story to instruct husbands, but even more profound is the instruction we receive concerning Christ, the husband of his church.

Questions for Consideration
1. Describe the basics of literary analysis.
2. Does literary analysis neglect theology?
3. How is the Bible like art?
4. What are some helpful questions we ask as we read biblical stories?
5. Does this approach undermine the basic authenticity and authority of the Scriptures?
6. What is irony, and how is it used in the book of Ruth?
7. What are some of the basic themes in the book of Ruth?

Lesson 3

Famine in the House of Bread

Ruth 1:1–2

All good stories are generally divided into three basic parts: a problem, an unraveling, and a solution.[1] Following this pattern, Ruth's narrative has an opening scene that introduces us to a genuine predicament. As the story begins, we encounter a man who takes his family to Moab because there is a famine in Bethlehem of Judah. He and his sons die in Moab, leaving his wife and eventually his daughter-in-law, Ruth, to return to Bethlehem. When they return, Ruth meets Boaz, and he fulfills the role of kinsman-redeemer. What begins as a tragedy of death and sorrow ends in the birth of new life and the resurrection of hope for the family of David. What a great story! But it gets even better! There is so much more to this story than merely the people in it—this story is the story of the gospel.

Some commentaries on Ruth maintain that the initial setting provides a backdrop to the story and nothing more. However, there appears to be far more than meets the eye.

"Now it came to pass, in the days when the judges ruled, that there was a famine in the land" (Ruth 1:1). The stage is set, and it is packed with redemptive meaning. That is to say, the setting has redemptive or covenantal significance. For example, the opening lines point us back to the book of Judges and one of the recurring themes in that book. Note Judges 21:25: "In those days there was no king in Israel; everyone did what was right in his own eyes." Ruth is the

---

1   Sinclair Ferguson, *Faithful God*, 21.

perfect story of transition—as the book of Judges concludes, Ruth's story begins. What happens in the story is coupled together with the problem of a famine. The author, Samuel, has a covenantal perspective as he links us to Judges. Therefore, when we read that it is the times of the judges and we also see that there is a famine in the land, we are confronted with a setting that is charged with theological/ redemptive meaning. The famine in the land informs us about more than the climate; it awakens us theologically to the unfaithfulness in the land.

When we read the Bible, we should expect to be taught the way of the covenant. This means that there is nothing random about the construction of biblical stories. As noted in the introduction, biblical narratives have redemptive or covenantal structure. This means that we can find redemptive theology or theological concepts not only taught explicitly but also embedded in the very structure of the text. For instance, the structure of Judges begs us to ask about the future. As we read the stories, we cry out in frustration and desperation, asking, "Who will free the people of God from this vicious cycle of failure and death?" "Who will be the judge that does not fall as Samson fell?" "Who will come without the frailty and weakness of Gideon?" Ruth's story provides a beautiful answer in the context of this agonizing cycle of failure. However, in Ruth we are pointed to the need for more than a judge; there is a need for a faithful husband. We are connected theologically with the last verse of Judges as it unfolds in Ruth.

Irony

Samuel uses irony as his most important device for deepening our meditation on Ruth's story. I have already noted that irony occurs when something that usually means one thing is deliberately twisted or changed so that it transmutes into the opposite. Samuel does this not just once or twice; he layers the whole story with irony. When we read it, we can peel back these layers of irony so as to deepen our appreciation of God's grace and mercy to the needy. What a delight it becomes to experience the layers of irony unfolding into a beautiful story that breathes with love, life, and hope!

Famine

Ruth's story begins with a stark opening sentence that is intended to alarm us as we read it—there was a famine in the land. To an ancient Israelite, the idea of famine in the land confronted them with a theological challenge. Famine provoked the faithful person to inquire, "How could there be famine in the land that was supposed to be flowing with milk and honey?" Of course, as we will see as we read it, this becomes even more ironic because the story is set in Bethlehem.

The land of Israel was God's gift as a place of rest and blessing. Thus, there was something covenantal about a famine in the land. The only time the land was dry was during times of curse. This reminds us to be sensitive readers of the way God was teaching his people in the days of Ruth. When the people turned away from God, he turned away from them. He turned his back on them, and in so doing, he dried up the land.

The Promised Land, which was supposed to be characterized as a fruitful land, is now described as dry. Thus, the first character in Ruth's story, Elimelech, is confronted with more than merely the problem of feeding his family; he has a covenantal choice set before him. To use a food metaphor, the table is set for a choice that will determine the course of the story. Will he respond with repentance and humility, or will he seek blessings outside the land? He can respond out of a sense of fear and desire for food, or he can respond out of a sense of faith.

Elimelech responds with fear and flight.

We are not told how long Elimelech may have waited before he made his fateful decision. But, given his subsequent actions, we have no problem understanding that his final decision was more closely connected with food than with faith. Samuel does not record that Elimelech sought repentance—instead he searched for other places of blessing; he left the Land of Promise.

One may rightly ask why we would criticize this poor fellow for trying to get his family some food. Why shouldn't he leave the land to find food? We answer this question with a reminder that Israel was under God's command to remain in the land as part of their call to be faithful. So God says in Deuteronomy 4:1, "Now, O Israel, listen to the statutes and the judgments which I teach you to observe, that you may live, and go in and possess the land which the LORD God of your fathers is giving you." Moses reiterates to the people of God that they must not only remain in the land He gives them, but they must occupy this land in spite of dreadful obstacles. If they were not faithful to this task, they would be tested even more severely and called back to faithfulness. Thus, we know that in redemptive stories famines are not random. When famines strike the land, they are not the result of a bare meteorological phenomenon. This is the modern understanding of weather. But in Old Testament redemptive narratives, famines would come to the land as God cursed his people or tested them regarding their faithfulness. For whatever the reason in God's sovereign purposes, famines provided the context for a test of faithfulness. So we are forced to see the covenant connection between famine and the passages found in Leviticus 26 and Deuteronomy 28. Famine in the Land of Promise can mean only one thing; God is testing his people. Famine in the Old Testament is a call to repentance and to covenant renewal. In Leviticus 26 we read,

If you walk in My statutes and keep My commandments,
and perform them, then I will give you rain in its season, the
land shall yield its produce, and the trees of the field shall
yield their fruit. Your threshing shall last till the time of
vintage, and the vintage shall last till the time of sowing; you
shall eat your bread to the full, and dwell in your land safely
[which is exactly what we see later when Boaz the faithful
husband responds to God with faithfulness—remember
he lays down on a huge pile of harvest from the land].
But if you do not obey Me, and do not observe all these
commandments . . . I will break the pride of your power; I
will make your heavens like iron and your earth like bronze.
And your strength shall be spent in vain; for your land shall
not yield its produce, nor shall the trees of the land yield
their fruit (vv. 3–5, 15, 19–20).

The same pattern in the land is taught in Deuteronomy 28.

Now it shall come to pass, if you diligently obey the
voice of the LORD your God, to observe carefully all His
commandments which I command you today, that the
LORD your God will set you high above all nations of the
earth . . . Blessed shall be the fruit of your body, the produce
of your ground and the increase of your herds, the increase
of your cattle and the offspring of your flocks. Blessed shall
be your basket and your kneading bowl . . . But it shall
come to pass, if you do not obey the voice of the LORD your
God, to observe carefully all His commandments and His
statutes which I command you today, that all these curses
will come upon you and overtake you . . . Cursed shall
be your basket and your kneading bowl. Cursed shall be
the fruit of your body and the produce of your land, the
increase of your cattle and the offspring of your flocks
(vv. 1, 4–5, 15, 17–18).

As they lived in the Land of Promise, if the people of God
were not faithful, God would bring famine. Ruth places us
in the middle of a scene of covenant testing. Elimelech faces
a test. Where will he turn to find food for his family? What

will he do? Through the famine, God calls Elimelech to make choices about his family's future.

Abraham had been faced with similar choices, and God had used a famine to challenge him. In Genesis 12, God tested Abraham's faith in his promises. Would Abraham believe that God would provide for him and protect his wife to whom God had given a promise of future blessings? You can almost feel the trembling in his voice as he pleads with his wife to pretend to be his sister. When Abraham responded in fear rather than in faith, his choices were so bad that even an Egyptian king rebuked him: "What is this you have done to me? Why did you not tell me that she was your wife? Why did you say, 'She is my sister'? I might have taken her as my wife. Now therefore, here is your wife; take her and go your way" (Gen. 12:18–19).

Elimelech faced the same kind of choice that Abraham faced. The structure of the Hebrew in our story is similar to that of Abraham's story. Would he trust in God's promise to provide food for his family in the land, or would he leave in fear? He was not a faithful husband. The Word of God required him to hold fast to the promises and thus to seek the restoration of the land.

Elimelech chose to leave the land and to seek food from other fields. He deliberately sought blessings outside of the land and thus outside of the covenant. He took his family away from the covenant and proved to be an unfaithful husband. Samuel immediately requires us to wrestle with the dire need of a faithful husband. How will this family survive without a faithful husband?

Some interpreters do not want to be so hard on Elimelech. For instance, Rabbi Ginsburg argues that Elimelech is really not the problem; his sons are the problem. He says this because the Hebrew that Samuel uses to describe Elimelech's action is the word for sojourning. This means, says the rabbi, that Elimelech was only on a temporary journey.

His sons, on the other hand, decide to stay or to dwell in Moab.[2] On one level the rabbi is exactly correct. We can be sure from this word that Elimelech had every intention of staying in Moab only temporarily. We can almost hear him telling himself and his family, "Look, I know that we shouldn't be doing this, but we will only stay until the famine has ceased."

The use of this word highlights for us the problem with trying to justify faithless living by saying that it will only be for a short time. Likewise, the foolish person who decides to live this way will soon discover the deadly character of such a decision. The word does mean something, but not exactly what the rabbi thinks. Rather, it points to the common problem of the progression of sins. That is to say, while Elimelech may have intended to stay only as long as the famine was in the land, his sons remained long enough to reap the consequences.

Certain decisions have a way of progressing to their natural conclusion. The very first psalm teaches us this in vivid images of walking, standing, and sitting. "Blessed is the man who walks not in the counsel of the ungodly, nor stands in the path of sinners, nor sits in the seat of the scornful; but his delight is in the law of the LORD, and in His law he meditates day and night" (vv. 1–2). The psalmist maps out a common progression in the life of sin. Sin has a way of making progress in our lives even if we start in rather small ways. We may only intend to walk somewhere for a brief time. Then we find that such ways become comfortable, and so we stand or linger in them. The next thing we know, we find ourselves sitting in the seat of the fool. Then the progression of sin is complete. James illustrates the progression in the following way: "When

---

2   Eliezer Ginsburg, *Mother of Kings: Commentary and Insights on the Book of Ruth* (Brooklyn: Mesorah Publications, 2002), 10.

desire has conceived, it gives birth to sin; and sin, when it is full-grown, brings forth death" (1:15).

We should never have taken that one step in the direction of sin. Elimelech's actions are an apt illustration of this principle. He intended to leave the Promised Land briefly in a time of famine, but his sons decided to live in the foreign land. We can even imagine Elimelech explaining his apparently unfaithful choice to leave the land of God and spend time in Moab, but only until the famine is over. "Then," he might say, "we will return to the Land of Promise." But sadly for his sons, *then* never comes, and they die in Moab. "A baby viper," says the old Puritan preacher, "will soon grow into a large snake if you let it live—so don't let it live for one second, but kill it quickly."

Heightened Irony

> And a certain man of Bethlehem, Judah, went to dwell in the country of Moab, he and his wife and his two sons (Ruth 1:1b).

Ruth opens with some dramatic flair, which heightens the irony. For instance, Samuel opens the story without naming Elimelech. You may not even notice this at first, but the very first man in the story remains unnamed. He says, "a certain man of Bethlehem" went to sojourn away from the land. This man, who is yet unnamed, left the Land of Promise. This seems to be designed to provoke some questions in our minds. For example, one might wonder, "Who is this guy anyway? Surely this poor fellow doesn't understand the covenant." The unnamed man is certainly one who doesn't acknowledge that God is King. Yet we are about to learn that the man who acts contrary to faithful service actually has a name that means *God is King*; he acts in complete opposition to his name. The man whose name means God is my King decided to reject the way of the King, leaving the land of life and blessing for a journey to a land of certain curses.

Moab

> And they went to the country of Moab and remained there (1:2b).

Samuel uses the literary setting to highlight for us that matters for this man are about to go from bad to worse. This faithless man journeys to the worst possible place one can imagine as it relates to the hope for bread, to the land of Moab.

Samuel's use of setting is powerful as he highlights the inevitable problems that Elimelech will have. It reminds me of a horror movie in which the setting lets everyone know that something terrible is inevitable. Movie directors use this kind of setting to heighten the tension of a story. For instance, a story might place us in a setting where a young woman is alone in a huge, creepy house on a dark and stormy night. The thunder is clapping outside, and the wind is howling. Suddenly she hears a strange noise in the basement. Of course, as she squeaks open the door to the basement, the electricity suddenly goes off. Hearing the strange noise again, she pauses for a moment to look curiously into the darkness below, and yet oddly she slowly begins to make her way down the stairs into the dark cellar beneath her. The potentially deadly character of the unknown noise does not dissuade her, even though everyone watching or reading her story already knows her fate. If she goes down into the darkness, she will meet a certain doom. The only person that does not seem to know her fate is the loony girl in the story. Everyone else who is watching can see it, and some people even begin to cover their eyes. Someone else may sense the tension so much that they yell out at the movie screen in an attempt to warn her from going down the stairs. Authors use this kind of setting to heighten the tension of a story. Ruth's story has exactly this kind of setting as it regards the covenant.

As sensitive readers, we can learn in covenant history that there are certain places one should never go for bread. As Elimelech searches for bread, he goes to Moab, the worst place in the world to look for bread. Why was this the worst place to look for bread? Moab was characterized as the place of famine for Israel; Moab was known for withholding bread from Israel. The land of Moab had been a consistent place of curse for the people of God. We read in Deuteronomy 23:3–4,

> An Ammonite or Moabite shall not enter the assembly of the LORD; even to the tenth generation none of his descendants shall enter the assembly of the LORD forever, because they did not meet you with bread and water on the road when you came out of Egypt, and because they hired against you Balaam the son of Beor from Pethor of Mesopotamia, to curse you.

We should meditate on this just a bit. Moab was a place of cursing for the people of God. Why do we know this? Because Moab was known for its refusal to feed Israel bread. Moab was the nation that actually hired Balaam to curse the Israelites. Knowing redemptive history, Elimelech should have understood this. Yet we see that the place known for refusing Israel bread is the very place he chooses to move his family for bread. Elimelech makes a self-destructive decision when he leaves Bethlehem, the house of bread, and seeks bread from Moab.

Moab and Her Daughters
There is yet another irony in Elimelech's choice of Moab. The Moabites were known for their evil and for their false worship. They worshiped the god Chemosh, and apparently even offered this god human sacrifices (see 2 Kings 3:27).

Not only were they renowned for their immorality in general but they also had an infamous place in redemptive history. The Moabites had resorted to more than one way to curse and to destroy the Israelites. At first they hired Balaam to curse Israel. However, when that did not work, they turned to a different method. Do you recall what that method was?

If you see what happens to Elimelech's sons, you will remember Moab's method of destroying Israel. They attempted to destroy Israel by getting them to marry their daughters. It appears from redemptive history that the Moabites had deliberately schemed to intermarry with the Israelites in order to conquer them. In Numbers 25 we hear that the Israelites were beginning to fornicate with the Moabite women, and as a result God began to kill the men with a plague. In Numbers 25:1–3 we read, "Now Israel remained in Acacia Grove, and the people began to commit harlotry with the women of Moab. They invited the people to the sacrifices of their gods, and the people ate and bowed down to their gods. So Israel was joined to Baal of Peor, and the anger of the LORD was aroused against Israel."

When Elimelech began to pursue daughters for his sons, ironically, he went to a place cursed for this very action. He sought wives for his sons from the worst place in the world that a faithful Israelite could imagine, from Moab. This was the land in which God had already killed the men of Israel for the very same action. Should we be surprised now to read that the result of Elimelech's decision is death to his sons? We see how heedless it was for Elimelech to seek refuge in this land for the reasons that he did. He was clearly a faithless husband who led his family directly into the jaws of death.

Just as God had told the Israelites to remain in the land, He had also warned them about intermarriage with foreigners who may turn them to false gods. The faithful believer was never to be "unequally yoked together." The law had made this clear to God's people, using the illustration of yoking of a donkey with an ox.[3] Nobody would yoke a donkey with an ox, because one is smaller, and it wouldn't work. The law was there to remind them that they couldn't join together the clean with the unclean. Paul restates this law in 2 Corinthians 6:14–18:

> Do not be unequally yoked together with unbelievers. For what fellowship has righteousness with lawlessness? And what communion has light with darkness? And what accord has Christ with Belial? Or what part has a believer with an unbeliever? And what agreement has the temple of God with idols? For you are the temple of the living God. As God has said: "I will dwell in them and walk among them. I will be their God, and they shall be My people." Therefore "Come out from among them and be separate, says the Lord. Do not touch what is unclean, and I will receive you." "I will be a Father to you, and you shall be My sons and daughters, says the LORD Almighty."

Elimelech acted contrary to his name and to the lessons of redemptive history. Ironic step followed by ironic step, Elimelech as a faithless husband led his family into the yawning jaws of death.

Questions for Consideration

1. What do we mean when we say that the setting has redemptive meaning?
2. How does the phrase "in the days when the judges ruled" fit this idea?
3. What does the setting of a famine teach us?
4. What are some Old Testament passages that teach this?

---

3   Deut. 22:10.

5. How does this setting force Elimelech to make a choice?
6. Do you agree that this is a test of his faith?
7. Why was Moab such a bad choice as a place of hope?

Bethlehem: A New Direction for the Future

Ruth 1:2–6

Ruth is filled with indicators that God will restore his people from the grip of death and set them in a new direction of life for the future. Samuel weaves this theme into the fabric of the story of Ruth using even the city of Bethlehem as an illustration. We know now that Bethlehem is the house of bread, the place of our Savior's birth, but this was not always the case.

In Ruth's story, Bethlehem is permanently transformed from a place of considerable danger and doom to a place of blessing and hope as the house of bread. We first hear of Bethlehem, which is called Ephrath or Ephratha, in Genesis 35. This story associates Bethlehem with death. One of the most painful episodes in the life of the patriarchs is the account of the death of Jacob's beloved Rachel:

> Then they journeyed from Bethel. And when there was but a little distance to go to Ephrath, Rachel labored in childbirth, and she had hard labor. Now it came to pass, when she was in hard labor, that the midwife said to her, "Do not fear; you will have this son also." And so it was, as her soul was departing (for she died), that she called his name Ben-Oni; but his father called him Benjamin. So Rachel died and was buried on the way to Ephrath (that is, Bethlehem). And Jacob set a pillar on her grave, which is the pillar of Rachel's grave to this day (Gen. 35:16–20).

We see Bethlehem associated here with ruin and death

as it marks the spot of Rachel's grave. Far from a house of bread in the early stories of redemptive history, Bethlehem had been associated with events that led to ruin and to demise.

Bethlehem is associated with the agony of the curse as Jacob's firstborn son betrays him and disgraces his father and family. So we read in Genesis 35:21–22, "Then Israel journeyed and pitched his tent beyond the tower of Eder. And it happened, when Israel dwelt in that land, that Reuben went and lay with Bilhah his father's concubine; and Israel heard about it." Moses tethers this city together with misery and disgrace, making it a place of defilement and contempt. Thus, early in redemptive history the city suggests misery, hardship, and pain.

This was the city of death and betrayal as recorded in Judges 17:7–13:

> Now there was a young man from Bethlehem in Judah, of the family of Judah; he was a Levite, and was staying there. The man departed from the city of Bethlehem in Judah to stay wherever he could find a place. Then he came to the mountains of Ephraim, to the house of Micah, as he journeyed. And Micah said to him, "Where do you come from?" So he said to him, "I am a Levite from Bethlehem in Judah, and I am on my way to find a place to stay." Micah said to him, "Dwell with me, and be a father and a priest to me, and I will give you ten shekels of silver per year, a suit of clothes, and your sustenance." So the Levite went in. Then the Levite was content to dwell with the man; and the young man became like one of his sons to him. So Micah consecrated the Levite, and the young man became his priest, and lived in the house of Micah. Then Micah said, "Now I know that the LORD will be good to me, since I have a Levite as priest!"

This man was Jonathan, son of Gershom, son of Moses.[1]
Hence, the grandson of Moses was an unfaithful Levite
associated with the city of Bethlehem.

The city, then, was associated with unfaithful priests, and
the fruit of this city appears to be rotten:

> And it came to pass in those days, when there was no
> king in Israel, that there was a certain Levite staying in
> the remote mountains of Ephraim. He took for himself a
> concubine from Bethlehem in Judah. But his concubine
> played the harlot against him, and went away from him to
> her father's house at Bethlehem in Judah, and was there four
> whole months (Judg. 19:1–2).

This slave wife was called out of Bethlehem and now
turned away from her husband. She became unfaithful and
went back home to Bethlehem, and her husband went there
to get her. Here her father attempted to detain the Levite.
He kept detaining him and attempted to persuade him to
stay with them. Once more, therefore, we see Bethlehem as
a place connected with unfaithfulness, betrayal, and death.

In Ruth, Samuel records how God resurrected this city
into the house of bread. The story of Ruth serves as the
all-important historical fulcrum by which God resurrects
Bethlehem to its well-known status as a place of life and
bread. Hence, as Samuel develops the narrative of Ruth, he
begins with a city that in the past had an association with
anguish and distress, but that now is linked with life and
hope. This hope would not only come to the people of God
in Ruth, but this city would be the place of hope for the
bread that would come down from heaven.

The Parents' Names: Elimelech and Naomi

The name of the man was Elimelech, the name of his wife
was Naomi, and the names of his two sons were Mahlon

---

1 See Judges 18:30.

and Chilion—Ephrathites of Bethlehem, Judah (1:2a).

Not only does Samuel tell us the story of reversal in the fortunes of cities but he also uses names to teach us of the reversal of the curse on families. It is significant for us to remember that names in biblical narratives play a very important literary and redemptive role. In the case of Elimelech, the name heightens the irony of his actions as well as the reversal that occurs at the end of the book.

Elimelech's name means "God is my King." Did he live up to his name? Matthew Henry noted that his name acted as a rebuke because he was unfaithful and lived contrary to it.[2] Someone who had God as his King should have responded to the famine with humility and repentance on behalf of the land. Living with God as your King would provoke you to recognize the covenant nature of your predicament. Instead, Elimelech forsook the covenant, which was united so closely with the land. He left the land and pursued death. As we read the text with sensitivity to the covenant, we are able to see his self-destructiveness quite clearly. The story gives us plenty of warning, which Elimelech should have heeded. We immediately note the danger, while Elimelech walks headlong into destruction for himself and his family. So the irony of his faithless actions is heightened all the more. Elimelech should have been faithful to his name, "God is King," and he should have tried to turn the city towards repentance. The painful consequences to his family are obvious.

Naomi is Elimelech's wife, and her name means "pleasant." Her name indicates a life of hope and delight. She is the bride to whom her husband should have been faithful. With names that mean *God is King* and *pleasantness* you might expect this couple to be the picture of fruitfulness and hope. Elimelech had the perfect name for

---

2   Matthew Henry, *Commentary on the Whole Bible*, vol. 2.

his calling to be a faithful husband. His task was to lead his wife in the way of life that provides her pleasantness. Yet he led her away from hope—he was not a faithful husband. So Naomi, whose name calls her to expect pleasantness, finds herself led into a time of bitterness.

The Two Sons' Names: Mahlon and Chilion
The names of Elimelech's two sons are also given in verse 2: "And the names of his two sons were Mahlon and Chilion—Ephrathites of Bethlehem, Judah." Here again emphasis is placed on their connection with Bethlehem, and in particular with Bethlehem as the ancient city Ephrath. These two sons were associated with Ephrath, and their names, which may have been Canaanite, indicate their expected lot. The first son mentioned is named Mahlon, which seems to mean "sickness" or "weakness." The second son, named Chilion, has a name that means "pining away," "failing," or even "annihilation."[3] Their names act as an eerie forecast of the coming doom for this family.

Samuel uses irony to name Elimelech's sons as he points to their destiny. Since their father has forsaken the covenant, their fate is a grim one. Hence, the author designates them as "weak" and "pining away." The birth of sons might normally forecast a hope for the future, but this story points to something entirely different.

First, we should understand that in biblical literature the names of characters are used as part of the literary structure. The author uses this structure to teach us redemptive lessons. Although a missionary recently told me of an African woman who named her daughter Malaria, we don't commonly name our children for dreadful images that represent a gloomy future. For instance, we don't really think that Elimelech and Naomi named their sons

---

3 Atkinson, *The Message of Ruth*, 35.

weak and pining away, do we? No, they probably initially gave them names that they thought were appropriate. According to Richard Pratt, "Old Testament stories differ from much world literature in their lack of attention to external appearance; physical descriptions occur only occasionally . . . These clues for characterization occur so infrequently that they deserve special attention when they appear."[4] Here Pratt was referring primarily to the external details of a story, such as height and weight. However, the same attention should be given to the names of biblical characters. Samuel gives us more than subtle hints as to the character of the personalities who are involved in our story.

Like much of biblical literature, this particular story uses names and name changes to teach us redemptive lessons. While we are used to names being used in positive ways, here the text uses names for negative instruction. Back to an earlier point, these people did not originally name their children *weak* and *pining away*. Rather, the author gave them story names or names that match their significance in the covenant. This is a very common teaching tool in biblical stories. It is not allegory in the purest sense, but we see that names are chosen to point us to the covenant significance of the characters. Also, God is the one who changes names in his sovereign power, indicating that he alone has sovereignty over men.

In other stories, for instance, we see the covenant significance of Abram, whose name was changed to Abraham. Jacob's name was changed to Israel. Saul's name was changed to Paul. Jesus changed Simon's name to Peter. We simply don't expect that Elimelech and Naomi were holding their precious sons in their arms, thinking of names

---

4   Richard L. Pratt, *He Gave Us Stories: The Bible Student's Guide to Interpreting Old Testament Narratives* (Nashville: Wolgemuth & Hyatt, 1990), 137.

to use, and happily called one of them *weakness*. No, these are their covenant names in the story.

We may not be as comfortable with name changes that are negative. Furthermore, we are probably not as comfortable with name changes that occur before we are even able to ascertain the original name. This does happen elsewhere. For example, if you read 2 Samuel 2:8 and 1 Chronicles 8:33, you will find that one of Saul's sons was named *Ish Bosheth* in the Samuel passage and *Ish Baal* in the Chronicles account.

Ish Baal means "man of the master," and the Chronicles passage calls him *Ish Baal*. The word Baal originally simply meant lord or master. This would mean that *Ish Baal* was "God's man." Certainly Saul named him a noble name that indicated his commitment to God. However, the name Baal began to contain negative connotations connected to the false worship of Baal. Hence, *Ish Baal*, which started as an inoffensive title, and indeed an excellent title, was changed to correspond to the change of connotations connected to Baal and rebellion to God. The name was consequently changed from *Ish Baal* to Ish Bosheth. This change clues us to the negative connotations associated with Ish Bosheth and his rebellion against God's anointed one, David. Ish Bosheth, in his rebellion against God, was a shameful man who brought shame to his father's house.

The same thing occurs with another of Saul's descendants, Mephibosheth, which means "from the mouth of shame." Certainly we can surmise that Jonathan did not name his son "mouth of shame." No, Samuel ascribes a name that carries a redemptive/theological meaning. Hence, the person 1 Chronicles 8:34 refers to as *Merib-Baal* is the same person Samuel refers to as Mephibosheth. *Merib-Baal* seems to have originated in the idea of "hero of Baal." The parents hoped the son would become a hero of the Lord. However, as Saul and his descendants brought shame to the line, the one who was originally named "hero of God" is now one who stands as a mouth of shame. Indeed, what a beautiful story unfolds in the kindness of David in 2 Samuel 9. Samuel's record of the kindness of David is heightened as we are reminded of the shame of the house of Saul. What a grand reversal occurs with the lovingkindness of King David! The household rightly titled with the shame of unfaithfulness and rebellion is mercifully restored from worthlessness and shame to the table of the king. Samuel uses the names of Saul's descendants to unleash the richness of God's mercy to those who come before him and recognize the reality of their shame. Surely Jesus' grand act of redemption is foreshadowed in this sweet story of a helpless descendant of Saul. And for our study of Ruth, we should note the importance of the name changes, which heighten our insight.

The use of name change to indicate theological meaning should not surprise us. Indeed, Naomi, whose name means pleasant, tells us herself about a name change. She will, through the author of the story, tell her people that she should no longer be called pleasant but bitter. Therefore, Samuel ascribes the names of *weakly* and *pining away* to the certainly cursed sons of Elimelech. Because of the unfaithfulness of Elimelech, these two young men are consigned to a life of languishing weakness. Does this not provide rich insight into all those who wander from the way of life? Those who stray from the hope of the covenant essentially consign themselves to a life of languishing desperation. The story tells us that their future will be one of suffering and gradual demise.

Elimelech Died: The Story Begins with Death, Death, and More Death

> Then Elimelech, Naomi's husband, died; and she was left,
> and her two sons. Now they took wives of the women of

> Moab: the name of the one was Orpah, and the name of
> the other Ruth. And they dwelt there about ten years. Then
> both Mahlon and Chilion also died; so the woman survived
> her two sons and her husband (1:3–5).

Naomi, the bride of the covenant, is now stranded by
her supposed protector.[5] Her husband is gone, her sons are
gone, and her future is gone with them. Elimelech, who
was called to be a faithful husband, has caused his wife to
be stranded in a foreign land, and God has brought them
to their painful but expected end. Naomi is now a helpless
widow. Here the story provokes us to question the future.
What will happen to the bride of this unfaithful husband?

The Hope of the Coming Faithful Husband

At this point in the story, a great transition begins to take
place, as Ruth moves into the story and acts in the place
of Naomi. The future of the covenant is going to belong
to Ruth. Naomi has a dead husband, dead sons, and a
dead womb. There is no hope for Naomi. The bride of
the covenant has been abandoned, and the scene is utterly
desolate and completely hopeless. The story now takes a
dramatic turn toward Ruth. This beautiful, young woman
steps forward and takes the place of Naomi as the bride
of the covenant. Because she is faithful, the future belongs
to Ruth. Hence, Samuel turns the reader's attention to this
beautiful, faithful young woman.

Ruth is young and has the hope of a husband as well
as the hope of a living womb. Ruth will be the one who
will have a son. We still see an obvious obstacle, and
Samuel directs us to the stark reality that without a faithful
husband, there is no hope, even for the vibrant, young
Ruth. The husbands who started this story are all dead.

---

5 Jim Jordan, "The Book of Ruth" (Biblical Horizons, Niceville, FL,
   1982), audio tape #2.

Hence, it is necessary for the bride to be taken by a younger brother who would act the part of the levir.[6] Yet, because Naomi is too old to remarry and have a younger son, their plight appears to be hopeless. Indeed, humanly speaking, their story is dead.

How can there be a faithful husband who will lead them into the way of the covenant when they are all dead? The reader is forced to conclude that the only hope for new life in this story will come from God, who must somehow provide a faithful husband. Their eyes and the eyes of everyone who reads this story are pointed forward to the hope of the coming of the faithful husband—one who will bring life to the dead.

The story causes us to cry out for someone to replace the death in this story with new life. We long for someone to do what the first husband in this story refused to do. A faithful husband would never have taken his family to the land of Moab. Elimelech's devastating choices have ruined his family and left them dead and hopeless. If there is going to be hope in our story, there must be a husband who will be faithful where the past husband has failed. So we see Samuel developing the story to the coming of Boaz as a type of Christ. The imagery is as beautiful as it is obvious. Just as Adam died in his unfaithfulness, so also Elimelech died, and his descendants with him. However, there is still hope in the coming of a faithful husband, Jesus the Christ. You see how the theme of Christ, the covenant, and redemption are replete in this story. They are woven beautifully into the very fabric of the text. The bitterness of unfaithfulness will be turned into the joy of new life through the true husband, Jesus the Christ.

So many of us are like Elimelech searching for bread in

---

6   See Deuteronomy 25:5–10 for the origin of levirate marriage, and see chapter 10 for a full discussion.

Moab. This is the place of dryness and death. This is the place of weakness and wasting away. Doesn't this remind you of the story from John 6, where the people followed Jesus for food and not faith? Like Elimelech, they went from place to place looking for food; they wanted bread, but they didn't want to find it in the place of God's command.

So often we do what the songwriter says when we "look for love in all the wrong places." We look desperately, but we will never find it, because it can only be found in the house of bread, in Jesus. We are all faced with the same kinds of questions that Elimelech faced. Where will we go for bread? Will we be motivated by food or by faith? As such, this story is also our story.

If we seek bread outside the city, we can expect starvation and death. If we expect this life to give us more than it can give us, then we will certainly find frustration. If a young person expects that college will give him everything he has been looking for, then he will find frustration. If you expect your job to give you a sense of satisfaction and fullness, then you will be disappointed in the end. You won't find nourishment for your soul in any other place than Bethlehem.

It is easy today not to learn from these stories. We look at the stories now and say with a real measure of confidence, "Well, if I would have been Elimelech, I would have stayed in Bethlehem." The most amazing example is that of the golden calf. We fail to appreciate this story's warnings because we say in our arrogance, "How could they have worshiped a golden calf after God had brought them across the Red Sea? How could they have forgotten the blessings of the Lord so quickly?" How could those Israelites have become grumpy so soon after leaving Egypt? They were given bread from heaven, and yet they complained. How could they do that? Then you should stop for a moment and ask yourself an even more important question, "How could a New Testament Christian be so lazy and ungrateful for the Bread of Life, Jesus Christ?"

It does not take too many of these kinds of questions to stir us to repentance and to faith. We quickly say, "Forgive us, O Lord, for being unfaithful. Forgive us, O Lord, for being so easily distracted from the source of true bread, Jesus." Perhaps you are asking yourself these same kinds of questions and you also need to be refreshed in Christ, who is the Bread of Life. In a practical way, we are called to find refreshment in the bread that satisfies to eternal life every time we approach the Holy Communion. By faith, we discover that man does not live by bread alone, but by every word that proceeds from the mouth of God. We can come to the Lord in the hope of the only bread that satisfies— Jesus Christ.

Questions for Consideration

1. What was the city of Bethlehem like before the story of Ruth?
2. What do Elimelech and Naomi's names mean?
3. What are their son's names, and what do they mean?
4. Why are names important in Bible stories?
5. How do name changes function in Bible stories?
6. What role does death play in the story of Ruth?
7. Do you think it is common to read Old Testament stories with humility and empathy?
8. Do you recognize the call to Jesus in Ruth? Explain.

Sovereign Reversal

Ruth 1:7–9

Elimelech's family left Bethlehem in the middle of a famine for relief, but the story took a remarkable turn for the worse. Elimelech had led his family "from the frying pan into the fire." Within a few verses of our story, everyone but Naomi was dead! Elimelech was dead. Mahlon was dead, and Chilion was dead. There were no husbands to provide for the future—in this sense there was no future. The story forces us to wonder what will happen now. What can this family possibly do next?

The first dialogue of the story begins as the three women discuss their dreadful situation. The unfaithfulness of Elimelech had brought the expected (at least for the sensitive reader) consequence of death and hopelessness. Samuel wants us to feel the utter despair in their plight. If we understand their despair, we will be ready to appreciate the amazing grace of God. We will be thrilled to watch God's sovereign reversal as the faithfulness of God reverses the unfaithfulness of Elimelech.

Elimelech's faithless actions have brought him to the expected end, which puts the family and us as readers on the road to a series of sovereign reversals or "returns." These reversals culminate in the ultimate reversal up to this point, which is the conversion of Ruth.

Just as dramatically as things turned to death and to destruction, our story turns toward life and hope. Samuel emphasizes the radical reversal of the fortunes of the people using the word return. In fact, he uses the word return so

frequently that we might think he has gone too far. He
uses the word and the concept as part of the dramatic flair,
which forces us to recognize it. Sinclair Ferguson notes
that "this word is the Old Testament's main expression
for turning back to God's covenant grace and mercy—for
repentance, for conversion."[1]

What an amazing change in the events we are about to
witness! The reverse setting and reverse fortunes go together
with the reversal of the whole story. Ruth's conversion is
nothing less than the complete reversal of the entire story
toward a new direction, a new beginning, and thus, a new
hope. Because it is vital for us to appreciate what God is
doing in the story, we need to take note of the reversals
Samuel emphasizes. We move dramatically from death
toward life, from Moab to Bethlehem, and from famine
to harvest.

The reversal in chapter 1 is obvious, but it bears emphasis.
Naomi returns to the very place where our story began.
Notice that by the end of this chapter the story comes full
circle. This reversal echoes in the title of Dean Ulrich's book
on Ruth, *From Famine to Fullness*. Not only are we back
in Bethlehem but everything has been reversed in extremely
ironic and rather odd ways. First, Naomi says, she went out
full but has come back empty. Yet at the beginning when
they left for Moab, the city of Bethlehem was empty. As
she returns to Bethlehem, the city that was empty is now
full. At the beginning of the story, Elimelech's family left
when there was a famine; now they return at the beginning
of a harvest. What a radical reversal we see! Samuel
compels us to recognize that the nature of the reversal is
singularly God's work! This is a radical reversal that occurs
because God sovereignly engineers it in spite of Elimelech's
unfaithfulness. Though Elimelech had determined to go in

---

1   Sinclair B. Ferguson, *Faithful God*, 25.

the opposite direction, God sovereignly moved his family back to Bethlehem.

Samuel allows us to peek behind the scenes to see God's sovereignty at work in the life of someone we have not yet met—Boaz. We find out later in the story that Boaz's faithfulness in Bethlehem had apparently provoked the blessing of the Lord, while Elimelech's unfaithfulness provoked the curse of the covenant on the family of Judah. So in spite of Elimelech's deliberate sins, God had already been sovereignly working to reverse the consequences of those sins in an entirely different place, not at all related (humanly speaking), yet coupled together by sovereign design. Since God is the one who established David's family in the land, this would be very important for the people of David's kingdom to realize.

God's sovereign grace fills us with a combination of humility and confidence. He accomplishes his divine design in spite of David's faithless ancestors. It is as if God drags the family back, kicking and screaming, to Bethlehem. In particular, Naomi's complaining reveals the bitterness that she says is reflected in the new name she gives herself. She wants to be called *Mara,* which means "bitter." Regardless that God had rescued her from the jaws of death and destruction, Naomi was apparently not humbled before the Lord.

Naomi's Complaint

Although we know that God had reversed the situation for the purpose of blessings, we see yet another bit of irony, because Naomi interprets things in reverse of God's reversal. Naomi complains that God had reversed her pleasantness to bitterness, but in reality at the very center of her complaint, God was reversing the entire direction of her life towards true pleasantness and ultimate blessings. When we peel back some of the ironic layers, we uncover

covenantal theology at deeper levels of our story. What
Naomi now thinks is death will ultimately bring her life.
She may complain about God bringing bitterness, but this is
merely because—like her husband—she was *still unfaithful
at heart.*

Thus, our story is definitely at a turning point. We are in
the midst of serious problems, and we may ask, "What will
happen to the covenant promises of God in the face of such
unfaithfulness? Will they die? Will the line of David end
and the promise end with it?" If you read biblical stories
honestly, this is certainly not the first time you may have
asked this question.

Redemptive history is replete with the record of man's
unfaithfulness. There are many stories of men who are
unfaithful and who have provoked curses on themselves and
those around them. Over and over again in countless ways
we find men who are unfaithful, bringing themselves and
their families into truly terrible situations. Yet their plight
is consistently and lovingly reversed by God's sovereign
faithfulness. How many times have we seen this? How
many times do God's people bring themselves to the very
precipice of death and destruction? We can recall that when
it looked as if man's unfaithfulness had brought complete
ruin to the whole world, God gathered Noah and his family
into the ark and provided them salvation.

Moses failed and was unfaithful. The judges failed and
were unfaithful. The kings of Israel and Judah failed and
were unfaithful. They turned left when they should have
turned right, and they turned right when they should have
turned left. Yet over and over in the biblical stories we
see the unfaithfulness of man not only matched but also
completely reversed by the faithfulness of God.

At this juncture in Ruth, our story points us to the same
conclusion about unfaithful men. Almost everyone in our
story is dead; the men are all dead, and the family has no

hope for the future, because in terms of her child-bearing capacity, Naomi's womb is dead and unable to produce more men. In this sense, death reigns!

How will God provide salvation through the family of Judah if that line is now dead? We are forced to see the sovereignty of God at work as we ask common questions. How will God maintain his promises? From where will new life come to the tribe of Judah? It will not be from the most expected source, which is Naomi, but from a foreigner, Ruth the Moabitess. God will bring salvation from the most unlikely and humble of places; *ironically he will bring it from Moab to Bethlehem*—what a reversal!

This is yet another deeply ironic reversal in our story. Using a Moabite woman in our story is like Jesus' use of the Samaritan woman in Luke 10. You would expect Naomi, as an Israelite, as a child of the covenant, to come back to Bethlehem at harvest praising God for returning her to the land of fruitfulness and fullness. Instead, she complains bitterly about how *God*—not her former husband or her own actions, not even her sons and their actions (who still had been given a chance to repent and return to the land)—has cursed her and how *he* has made her bitter.

Naomi is bitter about her life. She is bitter about the loss of her husband, which is no small problem. Who will care for her now? Who will provide for her now without a husband? Since her place is now among the widows, she complains bitterly as someone without a husband, and thus without security or hope.

Yet this is precisely the place to which her own actions have brought her. Likewise, this is the exact place God wants her to be, so she (and we through her) may learn of God's tender love for the helpless. She has clearly forgotten that at the center of the covenant is God's promise of divine provision for the widow and orphan. As such, God draws our attention later to the tender heart of Boaz, who obeys the Lord by following the gleaning laws, which provide for the needy.

The place of the widow in the Bible is central to the themes of redemption. It is no coincidence that widowhood is consistently listed as characterizing the needy whom God loves. God is said to have his eyes on the widow and the orphan. It is also no coincidence that the first time the word *widow* occurs in the Bible is in Genesis 38. Yes, Genesis 38 is the story of Judah and Tamar, which is where our story has its roots. Instead of trusting the Lord for his future, Judah abused the widow Tamar. This is where the tribe of Judah crashed on the rocks of sin and lust and where David's ancestors ruined their legitimacy for the future. In Genesis 38, the tribe itself had become like a widow: "Then Judah said to Tamar his daughter-in-law, 'Remain a widow in your father's house till my son Shelah is grown.' For he said, 'Lest he also die like his brothers.' And Tamar went and dwelt in her father's house" (38:11).

Judah was fearful that his daughter-in-law was cursed and that she would curse his sons, two of whom had already died. Judah was abusive and unkind to the widow Tamar, and he thus acts contrary to the covenant. God, on the other hand, gives his people clear direction regarding kindness to the widow: "You shall not afflict any widow or fatherless child. If you afflict them in any way, and they cry at all to Me, I will surely hear their cry" (Ex. 22:22–23).

The widow and the orphan were pictures of a helpless person. They lacked the security and the protection that was commonly needed. Therefore, God consistently warns his people to give due regard to the needs of the widow and orphan. The widow possessed a position of special affection in God's economy:

> For the LORD your God is God of gods and Lord of lords, the great God, mighty and awesome, who shows no

partiality nor takes a bribe. He administers justice for the fatherless and the widow, and loves the stranger, giving him food and clothing. Therefore love the stranger, for you were strangers in the land of Egypt (Deut. 10:17–19).

We could cite verse after verse in the Old Testament that reveals a particular divine concern for the widow. This is of course no less true of the New Testament. Indeed, religion in the Old Testament and the New Testament is summarized in James 1:27: "Pure and undefiled religion before God and the Father is this: to visit orphans and widows in their trouble, and to keep oneself unspotted from the world."

The widow becomes a veritable picture of the kind of person whom God loves, the humble. God becomes a father to the fatherless and a husband to the widow. Here the theme of the faithful and unfaithful husbands is being plastered over every angle and aspect of our story in Ruth. The story begins with an unfaithful husband, and then the rest of the story moves us to the conclusion of how God, through Boaz, provides a faithful husband. God's provision of a faithful husband will resurrect the line of Judah from death. In this sense, we should see Christ in this story from the beginning to the end.

God is providing Naomi with hope through a future husband, and it is not because of her faithfulness and humility. The whole story turns towards a future hope because of God's tender concern for the humble. Here the irony resumes. Naomi's name means "pleasant," which has an ironic twist at first, but now she cries out that her name is Mara, or bitterness. This is also ironic because God is in the process of providing her with true pleasantness through a faithful husband, through a coming savior, or what our story calls the kinsman-redeemer. But at this time in our story, Naomi refuses to look forward to this redeemer with hope. She refuses to look forward to the hope of the Lord! Rather, Samuel uncovers her hard-heartedness in the dialogue that follows.

Dialogue

Beginning with verse seven we hear the first dialogue of the story. Up to this point we have heard only from our narrator. Ruth 1:8 initiates the first discussion, which seems to point to a new literary unit. Now we hear from them in their own words. In fact, for the rest of the chapter we hear only from the women of our story. Other than our narrator, there are no male characters speaking in this chapter. It is worth noting that the heroine of our story is a woman. We see that the story of salvation is as much for women and girls as it is for men and boys. The primary figures in the story of redemption are male, but there is a fundamental focus on women as well. Like Mary, the mother of Jesus, Ruth is a humble woman of faith. God uses the humility and faithfulness of such women to form the very foundation of our faith.

In the dialogue and discussion among the women, we also learn a good deal of theology. Even more pointedly, we are focused on Naomi and Ruth. Naomi's words are first, and they set the stage for the radical reversal that God is about to engineer.

Naomi's Complaint Continued

As she speaks to her daughters-in-law, she says, "May the Lord grant you pleasantness." She is determined to detach herself and leave the land of Moab, but she will not face the reality of her situation. In fact, we actually see her physically attempting to detach herself from these young women. We find a deep-seated bitterness in Naomi. Naomi blames God almost entirely for her lot, even though she is contributing to it. Notice that her words to her daughters-in-law contain a kind of implication against the Lord. She invokes the Lord's name:

And Naomi said to her two daughters-in-law, "Go, return each to her mother's house. The LORD deal kindly with you, as you have dealt with the dead and with me. The LORD grant that you may find rest, each in the house of her husband." Then she kissed them, and they lifted up their voices and wept (vv. 8–9).

She says, "The Lord deal kindly with you, as you have dealt with the dead and with me." Naomi reverses reality when she says, "May the Lord deal kindly with you," implying that the Lord has not dealt kindly with her. Naomi's complaint reveals a heart full of bitterness, and she harshly implies that the Lord has not dealt kindly with the dead or with her.[2]

The structure of Naomi's words implies a deep-seated bitterness. She says, "May the LORD grant you rest," leaving the impression that she thinks the Lord has not granted her rest. Naomi requests that the Lord would grant them peace with a husband, implying that she thinks the Lord will not provide her such peace or such a husband.

When you listen to her complaint, you discover that she is bitter and that she believes her trouble is the Lord's doing. Isn't this just like us so often? We act contrary to faith and then cry bitterly to the Lord at the mess we have made. We howl at the Lord, implying that he has made our lot bitter, when in so many cases, as with Naomi, God has actually worked to bring salvation, while we have done our level best to provoke death. Here God is actually working to drive Naomi back to the city of bread, and yet she fights him. She goes back, as we say, "kicking and screaming." Isn't this so common for us? We rush toward a wall of destruction, and we run straight into a place of harm; then we moan and cry as we wallow in the wounds we have

---

2   See audio sermons, "Ruth Chapter One: The Story Begins," by James Dennison.

created for ourselves. "Of course," we say, "the Lord just doesn't want me ever to get ahead financially," as we pull out the credit cards to pay for our dinner out.

As Naomi finds desolation in Moab, and as she realizes that there is bread in her homeland, she decides to go where there is food. She now heads back to Judah. As she leaves to return to the homeland, her daughters-in-law attempt to follow her to Bethlehem in Judah. As we mentioned earlier, Judah is under a curse for failing to maintain the levirate law. From Genesis 38 we recall the terrible story of incest and illegitimacy. Hence, Samuel is pointing to the coming restoration and redemption of the tribe of Judah through the levirate law that Judah had violated.

The two daughters-in-law are also heading to Judah, and, ironically, Naomi attempts to dissuade them. Naomi has not been a woman of faith, and she continues in faithlessness. Rather than encouraging these two young women in the hope of the covenant and the possible redemption in the land, she attempts to discourage them from the only hope they really have for finding true food.

Ironically, Naomi tells them that they should not come. In a stunningly hard-hearted push, she is trying to turn them back to the ways of death. She has, as we noted, a serious reality problem. At this point she can't seem to come to grips with her self-created hardships, and she improperly attempts to direct these two young women back to the path of death. We are not told exactly why she tries to keep them from coming with her, except that she seems so blurred with bitterness at God that she herself would not even be returning to the land of Judah, except for temporary food. One teacher aptly states, "This whole family has been characterized by food and not faith."[3] It was food and not faith that drove Elimelech to leave the house of bread. Now

---

3   Jim Jordan, "Ruth," audio tape #2.

it is also for food and not faith that Naomi is driven back to the land.

She reminds us of the Israelites who chased Jesus around the lake for more food after he had performed a miracle to feed them:

> Jesus answered them and said, "Most assuredly, I say to you, you seek Me, not because you saw the signs, but because you ate of the loaves and were filled. Do not labor for the food which perishes, but for the food which endures to everlasting life, which the Son of Man will give you, because God the Father has set His seal on Him." Then they said to Him, "What shall we do, that we may work the works of God?" Jesus answered and said to them, "This is the work of God, that you believe in Him whom He sent." Therefore they said to Him, "What sign will You perform then, that we may see it and believe You? What work will You do? Our fathers ate the manna in the desert; as it is written, 'He gave them bread from heaven to eat.'" Then Jesus said to them, "Most assuredly, I say to you, Moses did not give you the bread from heaven, but My Father gives you the true bread from heaven. For the bread of God is He who comes down from heaven and gives life to the world." Then they said to Him, "Lord, give us this bread always." And Jesus said to them, "I am the bread of life. He who comes to Me shall never hunger, and he who believes in Me shall never thirst" (John 6:26–35).

Naomi's bitterness drives her to a life of seeking food that perishes rather than seeking true bread from God through faith.

Questions for Consideration

1. How does Samuel use the word *return* to teach us?
2. Describe some of the "returns."
3. How does Naomi respond to God's sovereign reversals?

4. Give some biblical examples of God's faithfulness in reversing the unfaithfulness of men.
5. How does the idea of widowhood fit into our story?
6. How is Naomi still operating by the principle of "food, not faith"?
7. What role does bitterness play in Naomi's bad decisions?
8. How does John 6 help us to understand this story?

Lesson 6

No More Sons

Ruth 1:11–21

> But Naomi said, "Turn back, my daughters; why will you go with me? Are there still sons in my womb, that they may be your husbands? Turn back, my daughters, go—for I am too old to have a husband. If I should say I have hope, if I should have a husband tonight and should also bear sons, would you wait for them till they were grown? Would you restrain yourselves from having husbands? No, my daughters; for it grieves me very much for your sakes that the hand of the LORD has gone out against me!" (Ruth 1:11–13).

Naomi actually succeeded in dissuading one of her daughters-in-law from following her to the Promised Land. In her arguments she even had the audacity to pretend that the whole ordeal was worse for her than for them. Making reference to the levirate laws, she contended that even if she could bear a son, the two younger women would be too old by the time the sons could marry either one of them. Here she completely ignored the possibility of other family members who live in the land acting as husbands to them. Instead Naomi insisted on concentrating entirely on the deadness of her womb. She believes—and thus she acts as if—there is no hope for the future. Her thoughts are simple—her sons are dead, her womb is dead, and the future of her house is dead. We are reminded of the story of Genesis 38 and Judah's refusal to follow God by faith when his sons had died. Indeed, like Judah, Naomi tries to rid herself of a woman she believed was a curse.[1]

Naomi ruminates about the possibility of her bearing a son, but because she is too old, she concludes that this is impossible. She should have recalled redemptive history, because this would not have been the first time God brought miraculous life to the dead womb of an older woman. Even though God had changed these kinds of situations in the past, Naomi persists in her despair, and she drives Orpah away from the hope of the covenant. Furthermore, Naomi blames God for her despair while never assigning any responsibility for her plight to the unfaithfulness of her husband. She refuses to assign any guilt to her husband, even though he had attempted to provide for his family's future outside of the covenant. What a missed opportunity! She could have sought restoration as she confessed her sins; instead she blames God. Her situation was the accumulation of a series of ungodly decisions and faithlessness. Yet Naomi assigns the responsibility to God, telling her daughters-in-law to return to Moab to find husbands, which she now believes that neither she nor God can provide. In responding in this way, she indicates that she does not believe God will provide them with a future. Quite simply, she is not living by faith. This is a recurring theme in the story of Ruth.

Next we encounter a setting of profound emotions as Samuel narrates a gripping incident of weeping, wailing, and sadness. This scene is filled with the deep emotions of the moment. These women were touched with the hardest of life's trials and pains, and they realize that nothing will ever be the same for them. Thus, we see them clinging to one another, lamenting with genuine heartache and loss over this truly sad transition in their lives. If you have ever

---

1 See Dean R. Ulrich, *From Famine to Fullness: The Gospel According to Ruth* (Phillipsburg, NJ: P & R Publishing, 2007), 27.

had to say goodbye to a friend, or closer yet, to a son or daughter when they leave subsequent to life-changing event, then you know something of the emotion of this scene. This scene becomes one of the many critical turning points in our story.

Orpah Turns Back

As her daughters-in-law weep and cling to her, Naomi persists in pushing them back to Moab. Orpah, whose name probably means "fawn," reacts naturally, leaving Naomi and returning to her people. After all, since Naomi's God had mocked Naomi's name as the pleasant one and had refused to provide for her family, what hope would one expect for Orpah, a foreigner. Orpah may have properly noticed that the family's position was characterized by rootless wandering for food—hardly an enticing prospect for a foreign widow. Just as their sons' names had indicated, they found nothing but agony and a gradual languishing. Naomi's testimony of the cruelty of God had its intended effect. Orpah listened to the bitter words of Naomi, and she decided to return to Moab.

In striking contrast, Ruth did not despair. Once Naomi convinced Orpah to return, she concentrated her full efforts on persuading Ruth to leave her. Ruth 1:15 rightly tells us the nature of returning to Moab. We read, "And she said, 'Look, your sister-in-law has gone back to her people and to her gods; return after your sister-in-law.'" If you think about the theological import of what Naomi was trying to do, you realize that she was a terrible witness! A sensitive reader will discover that this was not merely a return to the fields of Moab, but a return to the gods of Moab.

Ulrich rightly notes, "By sending Orpah and Ruth back to their gods, Naomi broke the first commandment and denied its practical application to a specific case...The one true God was allegedly not sufficient to grant security to all who trust in him, regardless of national and social background."[2]

Naomi was arguing vigorously to push these women to their assured doom. Imagine an Israelite from Bethlehem having become so bitter that she tries to push her daughters-in-law away from the Lord! Naomi's arguments were an attempt to lead them to their eternal death. At this point, we can give great thanks that the future did not depend on Naomi!

Ruth's Conversion

In the midst of this intensely emotional scene, something dramatic emerges; Ruth refuses to leave. In fact, Naomi cannot detach Ruth from her, because she clings to her and refuses to let go. She holds so tightly that at this point she becomes the only person in our story who sees with the eyes of faith. Surprisingly, Ruth (not Naomi) interprets her decision to return to Bethlehem as a religious commitment to the Lord.

Ruth determines to follow the God of Israel and takes Naomi's place as the covenant representative of the family, just as Boaz will later take the place of Elimelech as the family's covenant representative. Now we have a foreigner refusing to fail, and Samuel portrays Ruth as an active contrast to Naomi and Orpah. She will not despair but holds tightly, embracing the covenant promises and looking to the future.

Naomi uses the pervasive word *return*. At first, both women promise to return, saying "our return will match your return." But Ruth determines to act with true faith. She clutches the covenant and embraces the faith that Naomi must have taught her when they first met. Ruth's grasping hold of the covenant promises of God provides

---

2   Ulrich, *From Famine to Fullness*, 32.

not only the reversal of the lot of foreigners such as Ruth but also the reversal of the entire city of Bethlehem, and through it, the whole world. What follows is perhaps one of most-quoted conversion experiences in the whole Bible. This is a confession of faith *par excellence:*

> But Ruth said: "Entreat me not to leave you, Or to turn back from following after you; For wherever you go, I will go; And wherever you lodge, I will lodge; Your people shall be my people, and your God, my God. Where you die, I will die, and there will I be buried. The LORD do so to me, and more also, If anything but death parts you and me" (vv. 16–17).

Ruth Joins the Pilgrimage

This passage continues in the vein of many Old Testament books regarding the theme of pilgrimage. The Bible characteristically portrays the history of redemption as a pilgrimage. God's covenant people are on a journey of faith. Indeed, the call of our father Abraham from Ur of the Chaldeans to the city of God is a pattern for the walk of faith for all of God's people. Ruth now chooses to join this journey with the covenant people of God. Ruth chooses to become a pilgrim to the house of bread, and this act of faith is what reverses the direction of our story and begins the new story of restoration and hope.

Ruth is a faithful bride, and God has now become her husband. Samuel provides us with a tangible, colorful picture of God's faithfulness to the widow. Now we see that there is still a future for God's people.

Covenantal: Your People Will Be My People

If you are either starting your pilgrimage or if you have been walking for a long time, Ruth's story is encouraging— no person ever walks the journey of faith alone. Ruth not only started a pilgrimage, she also joined a family. God

calls us out of darkness and into his glorious light in the
company of others. We join his covenant people, and we do
not do this as individuals. In the Bible there is no such thing
as individualistic salvation, and there are no "lone rangers"
in God's kingdom. Ruth herself makes this connection,
saying that Naomi's people will be her people, and thus she
becomes a part of the covenant community. Her destiny and
her future are wrapped together with the future of God's
community. Even as an "outsider," Ruth soon discovers
the blessing of covenant community. In this sense, Ruth's
confession of faith includes the confession of the "holy
catholic church." We are called to be covenantal. There is a
proper sense of connectedness in her confession.

In committing herself to the Lord, Ruth uses a covenant
expression as a vow or oath. We see this same thing in
Genesis 15, when God acts as the one who invoked a self-
condemning or a self-maledictory curse. This phrase, "may
the Lord deal with me," is a part of Ruth's covenant with
the Lord as well as with Naomi, as she invokes the name
of the Lord.

Buried in the Land

"Where you die, I will die and be buried." Here we may see
something of the land as a place of hope and resurrection.
When discussing the concept of famine, we noted that the
land was a place of hope and rest. It was, therefore, very
important to be buried in the land. The land represented
resurrection and hope for future rest. The land was a
symbol of the future Sabbath and resurrection life.

As Elimelech left the Land of Promise, he went into the
wilderness. He journeyed to Moab, a land characterized
by death for God's covenant people. Here again the irony
is amazing. In the Old Testament, God had established the
Land of Promise as the place where his name was exalted.
The land was the dwelling place of God. To be outside of

the land was to be outside the promise of the covenant. The land was holy to God; it was sacred. God had invested the land with powerful redemptive meaning. It was the place where he promised to dwell with his people. The land in some ways was like the garden of Eden. It was the place where God had promised peace and rest to his people.

In the Old Testament, since the land was the place of rest, it was considered the proper place of burial. Indeed, Moses devoted a large section of the Genesis account entirely to Abraham's negotiation and purchase of a burial plot for Sarah (Genesis 23). The father of our faith considered it very important to bury his family in the land. Jim Jordan states, "Abraham was a stranger and sojourner in life, but in death he was a stranger no longer. Hence, he actually owned this part of the land, and this was a down payment on possession of the whole of the land."[3]

This is not the only place in Genesis in which God makes it evident that his people should be buried in the Land of Promise. Jacob instructs his sons specifically:

> Then he charged them and said to them: "I am to be gathered to my people; bury me with my fathers in the cave that is in the field of Ephron the Hittite, in the cave that is in the field of Machpelah, which is before Mamre in the land of Canaan, which Abraham bought with the field of Ephron the Hittite as a possession for a burial place. There they buried Abraham and Sarah his wife, there they buried Isaac and Rebekah his wife, and there I buried Leah. The field and the cave that is there were purchased from the sons of Heth." And when Jacob had finished commanding his sons, he drew his feet up into the bed and breathed his last, and was gathered to his people (Gen. 49:29–33).

It is important to be buried in the Land of Promise.

3 Jim Jordan, "The Book of Ruth, chapter 1b," *Biblical Horizons* audio tapes.

Indeed, the next chapter in Genesis offers us great detail regarding Jacob's funeral and the trip to the land for burial. Furthermore, Joseph also underscores the importance of burial in the land: "Then Joseph took an oath from the children of Israel, saying, 'God will surely visit you, and you shall carry up my bones from here.' So Joseph died, being one hundred and ten years old; and they embalmed him, and he was put in a coffin in Egypt" (Gen. 50:25–26).

When we die, we go to God, and he is our dwelling place. When we die, we go to Abraham's bosom; we go to be with Christ. Today it no longer matters where we are buried in regard to a sacred space. In the new covenant, Christ is our ultimate place of dwelling. We are in Christ, and as such we no longer have a piece of land wherein we find rest or hope for resurrection in the future.

Unfortunately, in a number of Christian traditions this idea lingers in superstitious ways. Some traditions place a strong belief in "holy" places. Certain places are invested with special power as they are considered holy and sacred to God. This is why if someone is excommunicated from these churches, he loses the privilege of being buried on sacred ground. In fact, when the famous John Wycliffe died, he was in good standing and was buried on holy ground. However, after his death, he was excommunicated posthumously, and his bones were exhumed. After his remains were unearthed, they were burned as those of a heretic.

Old Testament literature taught that the land was the location where God had set his name as a sacred place, which God had set apart for holy use. Therefore, the land had a tremendous significance, and it mattered greatly where God's people were buried. In the Old Testament it was important to be buried in the land as a symbol of their hope of future rest, but this is no longer the case in the New Testament. When we die, we go to be with Christ. The

Scriptures inform us that to be buried in the land was to be asleep in the place where God dwells. It was to be asleep with the Lord. Now, of course, we sleep in Christ when we die, and in Christ we wait for the resurrection. Hence, even in the burial practices of the Old Testament saints, we are beautifully pointed to Christ and the hope of the resurrection.

In the Old Testament, the land was part of the promise of the covenant. God's land was sacred space. This would become even more specific when God built the temple. The land and the temple were the places where God promised to dwell with his people. In the new covenant, the church has replaced God's special covenant land. The people of God are the land today (see Heb. 12:22). The church is now the place where God has ordered His name to dwell. Thus, the church has replaced the land as the "place" of blessing. This is not to say that the actual parcel of earth upon which a church building is dedicated is sacred dirt. But rather, wherever God's name is named among His people, He has promised to dwell there in the midst of them. His covenant promises are no longer bound to a geographical location, but they are given to His body, the church.[4]

You can commonly see this concept perverted in horror movies in which sacred dirt or water or other objects are used to ward off evil things. Many of these perversions come from churches that continue to mix Old Testament and New Testament concepts improperly. Yes, the church is the holy land or dwelling of God. But this does not mean that church property has any more sacred value than farmland in Ohio.

A missionary to Ethiopia came to visit our church and showed slides of superstitious Christians who bowed down

---

4   See Edmund P. Clowney and Gerald Lewis Bray, *The Church* (Downers Grove, IL: InterVarsity, 1995), 44–45.

to kiss what they considered to be sacred holy stones. These stones were invested with special powers because of their connection to past spiritual wonders. The superstitious worship of stones and sacred places is testimony to the perversion of this Old Testament concept. In the New Testament, the Bible teaches that the whole earth is to become sacred, as the church goes into the world making disciples of its inhabitants. Now wherever God's people go, the land goes with them, because they are the place where God has placed His name.

Many prophetic or eschatological schemes still include strange concepts of the resurrection of a promised land, and they are utterly misleading. The land always pointed us to the place of rest within God's covenant, which ultimately is Jesus the Christ. The church as the dwelling place of God is now the land in the sense that this is the place where God has caused his name to be named; it is now the sacred place for God's people. This is true, of course, not in a geographic sense, but in a spiritual sense.

At this time in redemptive history, geographically speaking, there is no sacred space. Now the promises with respect to the land have been replaced, and the whole earth is made clean in the work of the church. Now, wherever God's people dwell, there the concept of sacred land is fulfilled—there is no sacred land in the same sense as there was in Ruth's day. Ruth's heart's desire points us to what our desire should be—we should want God to dwell with us forever. Christ has come as the dwelling place of God. Outside of Christ there is no hope of life. It was to this that the concept of the Land of Promise pointed, and to this Ruth testified in her statement that she longed to be buried in the land.

Buried in Bethlehem
Here we look at a minor but poignant image of Ruth as the

new Rachel. Ruth was asking to be buried in Bethlehem. She would become the fruitful bride and bear a child of the covenant. Hence, she would be like a second Rachel as a new bride of the covenant. In redemptive history, Bethlehem was the place where Rachel was buried, and this would be the place where Ruth would find a faithful husband and become the blessed bride of the covenant. She will take the place of Naomi as the new bride of the covenant.

> Now the two of them went until they came to Bethlehem. And it happened, when they had come to Bethlehem, that all the city was excited because of them; and the women said, "Is this Naomi?" But she said to them, "Do not call me Naomi; call me Mara, for the Almighty has dealt very bitterly with me. I went out full, and the LORD has brought me home again empty. Why do you call me Naomi, since the LORD has testified against me, and the Almighty has afflicted me?" (Ruth 1:19–21).

Naomi cries out against the Lord, revealing a deep bitterness against her God. She continues to blame the Lord for her circumstances, and she does not properly acknowledge any need for repentance for leaving the land or for giving her sons to Moabite women. Instead, she accuses God as the one who brought her to these woeful circumstances. Is this not characteristic of bitterness toward God? We sin and we rebel, but when the painful consequences begin to strangle us, we cry out in bitterness.

Naomi now asserts that her new name is *Mara* or "bitter." This also reminds us of Rachel's death in Bethlehem, when she named her son *Ben-Oni,* "son of sorrow." Rachel was essentially asking to be called "Mrs. Sorrow." Here Naomi seems to be doing the very same thing. Naomi is continuing in Rachel's footsteps of bitterness. As the story unfolds, Ruth will replace these women, and she will become a blessed bride of the covenant. Rachel died in bitterness, and Naomi has already expressed both her deadness and bitterness. The pattern of resurrection reversal is obvious. Resurrection through God's intervention is the only hope for the future—and this is exactly what will happen. Once the city of Bethlehem was cursed and Rachel died a sorrowful bride, but now God is reversing the scene and bringing new life to the city.

Samuel continues to use new life or resurrection as a consistent theme. Because God is faithful to his covenant, he will offer his people a new beginning. This is so characteristic of the hope of the covenant. At this juncture in Ruth, we have a new beginning—salvation comes as a new beginning. Salvation is the image of new beginning— the image of God bringing life from the dead. Consequently, salvation never comes from man. It always comes as God breaks into history from eternity and provides redemption. He brings hope to the hopeless and life to the dead. Noah was spared a certain death from the worldwide flood because God gave him new life. Abraham was called out of the city of death and into life with God. Israel was taken out of the land of slavery, and God brought them out to life. In Ruth we see yet one more of the many beautiful illustrations of this same "death to life" principle of redemption.

In Ruth's story, God is about to create new life from the dead womb of Naomi. The pages of redemptive history testify that the idea of God bringing new life from dead wombs is not new. Didn't God break through the death of Sarah's womb and provide resurrection life? This is yet another grand example of resurrection life to the dead womb. Naomi is dead, but Ruth will take her place and bear a son, Obed. Naomi adopts Obed, and once more salvation comes through resurrection.

Given Naomi's bitterness, we know that her actions will not be the basis of any hope. If it were left to the one whose name means "pleasant," there would be nothing but

bitterness. Yet the chapter ends with the hope of a harvest.
Though the chapter began with a famine, it now ends
with bounty.

Another common theme in Ruth is that of God raising
the hope of new life from a barren woman. God brings new
life from a woman in whom there is nothing but death. He
did this with our mother Sarah. He did this in answer to
the tearful prayers of our mother Hannah. He is doing this
through Ruth, who, like these others, becomes a paradigm
for the coming of our mother Mary.

The mother of our Lord is named *Mary,* which means
"bitter." This is the pattern of the Old Testament, in which
barren women, with faithfulness and humility, provoke God
to grant them new life. In one sense the whole old covenant
is a bitter experience, because people keep dying, and there
does not seem to be any hope. In Mary we have new life
or resurrection life coming from the womb of a virgin.
Ruth's book provides a pledge for the coming Servant of the
Lord who would be born in an unexpected way. Obed the
"slave" or "servant" is the son of Ruth, the Moabitess.

Scholars don't agree on the meaning of Ruth's name.
Some say the name Ruth means "a sight," "a companion,"
or "a female friend." Ruth was literally "a female friend"
and "a companion" to Naomi. The meaning of her name
is less important than the virtual title that Samuel gives
for her. One scholar argues that there is an unspoken
communal conspiracy not to mention the Moabitess.[5] Thus,
she is Ruth "the Moabitess." Her virtual title is the most
important part of her name—she is a foreigner! She was
from Moab, and this was the hallmark of who she was.

In fact, the text begins to make a transition. As it does
so, Samuel calls her "Ruth the Moabitess" for the first time

---

5 Ian M. Duguid, *Esther and Ruth, Reformed Expository Commentary*
(Phillipsburg, NJ: P&R, 2005), 144.

in the story. Yes, we already know that she is a Moabite, but she is given the title, "Ruth the Moabitess." She is connected to Moab in an ironic manner. As our earlier discussions noted, Moab was a noted land of curse. In particular, Moab was a place where the men of Israel were plagued because of the women they married. Our minds might certainly wander back to the roots of the family of Moab. Ruth's ancestors come from Lot's incestuous relations with his daughters, as we read in Genesis 19, "Thus both the daughters of Lot were with child by their father. The firstborn bore a son and called his name Moab; he is the father of the Moabites to this day" (vv. 36–37).

Our story is specifically connected to the childlessness of Tamar, the daughter-in-law of Judah, and the incest that ensued, and the apparent hopelessness that this brought (Gen. 38). Likewise, Ruth's origin is doubly ironic, because her cursed forefathers had their origin in the same kind of problem with childlessness, which was complicated by incest. Hence, Ruth's role as the bride of the covenant is even more ironic, given her origins.

There is layer upon layer of ironic hopelessness. Yet God, in his matchless mercy, peels back those layers with the power of the resurrection. Indeed, the layers of despair and hopelessness actually work to enhance the wonder of God's grace. God undoes what it is impossible for man to undo. God stands where it is impossible for man to stand. So the cross and resurrection are powerfully projected as man's only hope in the face of sin and death—only God can save.

There is such deep inspiration in this story. We may be covered with layer upon layer of sin and death, but the resurrection power of our Savior strips it of its power over us. "O death, where is thy sting?" says Paul. What seems impossible for man is easy for the God of the resurrection. The layers of irony should deepen our own appreciation of the compassion and power of God to bring life where there is nothing but death. Truly God brings hope to the hopeless and power to the powerless.

Questions for Consideration

1. Why does Naomi conclude that there is no hope for the future?
2. What was the religious significance of Naomi's attempt to send her two daughters-in-law back to Moab?
3. Why does Ruth refuse to leave?
4. How does Ruth join a pilgrimage? Does she join it alone?
5. Why would someone in the Old Testament want to be buried in the Promised Land?
6. How has this connection to the land changed in the New Testament?
7. How is Ruth like a second Rachel, and how does she point forward?
8. Explain the beauty of Ruth's status as a foreigner.

Lesson 7

God Provides a Redeemer

Ruth 2:1–3

In chapter 2, Samuel shows us the savior of the story, or better yet, we could say that God Himself provides a redeemer. Yes, every detail of this profound little story drives us forward to the coming encounter with the kinsman-redeemer, Boaz. I want to remind you that Boaz points us to the ultimate kinsman-redeemer, Jesus Christ. God combines his sovereign might with his sovereign mercy as he creates the absolutely perfect man to snatch Ruth from the jaws of death. There is nobody in all of Israel more perfectly fitted to rescue Ruth from her unique situation than Boaz. The most creative artist in the world could not have crafted a more beautiful, a more poignant, or a more perfectly suited husband than Boaz.

Elimelech's actions have provoked the expected results of death and confusion, and Samuel brings us to another important turning point in the story. From the chaos of the weakness and faithlessness of Elimelech, the Lord causes Ruth to emerge as the heroine. Naomi had resolved to return to Bethlehem for food, while Ruth had determined to travel to the city in faith. The Jewish characters from whom we might have expected hope in the Lord have failed miserably. Only Ruth, the foreigner, turns in faith towards the city of bread.

The common portrait of Ruth as sorrowful and forlorn simply does not match the biblical story. John Keats (1795–1821), for instance, in his famous poem *Ode to a Nightingale,* paints the all-too-typical picture of Ruth as haunted with sorrow and filled with despair.

> Thou wast not born for death, immortal Bird!
> No hungry generations tread thee down;
> The voice I hear this passing night was heard
> In ancient days by emperor and clown:
> Perhaps the self-same song that found a path
> Through the sad heart of Ruth, when, sick for home
> She stood in tears amid the alien corn;
> The same that oft-times hath
> Charm'd magic casements, opening on the foam
> Of perilous seas, in faery lands forlorn.

Many famous pictures and poems portray the young
Ruth as beautiful but forlorn, as young but woeful. She is
depicted as haunted with the sadness of loss and filled with
the despair of death—a despair that has driven her to a
strange and foreign land. As Keats notes, she is homesick
for Moab and, like the beautiful nightingale, sings a
charming but sad song that troubles the soul. According
to Keats, Ruth stood among the sheaves, homesick. This
imagery works well for art and creates excellent pictures for
poetry, but compared to the actual story of Ruth, it looks
like bad theology.[1]

The Bible actually paints a strikingly different portrait of
our strong, young heroine. Ruth is not forlorn but hopeful.
She is at a new beginning, and she finds joy in her Lord.
She is a new creature, and her life has a fresh new start. She
is not homesick, nor is she sad and pining for her former
life. To the contrary, Samuel portrays a fresh, hard-working
and joyful young woman who is vibrant and filled with
an unsullied sense of purpose and hope in the Lord. As
such, she leads the story forward for us. Unlike the foolish
Elimelech, who turned away from the house of bread for
food in the cursed land of Moab, Ruth turns to the fields of

---

1 James Dennison, *Ruth*, audio tapes.

Bethlehem, and, in so doing, she turns the entire story in a new direction. She turns to the Lord of Bethlehem in faithfulness.

While Naomi wallows in her bitterness, Ruth looks forward to the salvation of the Lord. Ruth is a vibrant, strong woman of devotion who sees with the eyes of faith. As such, she pulls the story forward with hopeful anticipation of the Lord's goodness. This is how Samuel draws us from the death and sorrow of Moab to the life and harvest of Bethlehem.

Boaz
Chapter 2 inaugurates a dramatically different scene. Our two widows have come to Bethlehem at the beginning of the barley harvest, and a new man enters the picture. Samuel writes of an obvious change in the fortune of these two women that hinges on this new man, Boaz. He introduces us to Boaz, but in a way that draws or pulls us forward in the story toward the "hoped-for" center where Ruth and Boaz meet—and what a great meeting!

Everything about the new setting corresponds to the theme of resurrection. As sensitive readers, we must observe that the scene in Bethlehem undergoes a marked change from the beginning of the story. Bethlehem has now been transformed from famine to harvest, and Boaz is at the heart of these changes—apparently he has been the one who made a difference in the city. The city is now a place of bread, and Boaz is deliberately connected to revival and to harvest. It is into this wondrous scene that Ruth enters the city.

Samuel uses the harvest to mark yet another fundamental turning point in our story. The barley harvest was the first of the cereals to be harvested, probably around April. This harvest, along with the wheat harvest, came to be identified with the festivals of Passover and Pentecost—times of

celebration and praise. Harvest marks not only the blessing
of Bethlehem, but connected with it, it marks the beginning
of restoration or resurrection for Naomi. Harvest, then, has
an appropriate *resurrection* connection. Our dead family
returns to the land and is immediately confronted with
the hope of harvest and resurrection. This is exactly what
happens as the story unfolds.

God Provides a Savior

> There was a relative of Naomi's husband, a mighty man of
> valor from the family of Elimelech whose name was Boaz.

In Ruth 2:1, Samuel tells us that Naomi had a relative,
but at this point he is unknown, and we do not know that
he is a near kinsman—merely a relative. Samuel's vague
description of our new man is like the description of chapter
1:1, "A certain man of Bethlehem of Judah." However,
our new man is described as a mighty man of valor. This
phrase, mighty man of valor, usually refers to someone
mighty or outstanding as a warrior. Some translations say
that he was a "man of great wealth." It is also important to
note the King David will later be called an *ish gabor hiyel*
or "mighty man of valor." According to André LaCocque,
"The parallel with David's dynasty is not mere chance."[2]
Samuel subtly makes the connection between the mighty
man Boaz and his descendant, King David.

Boaz was certainly a man of great wealth, but his wealth
is not emphasized in the story. Rather, Samuel points us to
Boaz's role as a powerful man of the city—not to his wealth
per se. He was an influential and vital man in Bethlehem.
His connection with David's dynasty and the coming
harvest is powerful in many ways; the connection is also

---

2 André LaCocque, *Ruth: A Continental Commentary* (Minneapolis:
Fortress, 2004), 62.

eschatological because it speaks of the future.[3]

Boaz was the ruler or judge of the city. If not in title, yet certainly in fact, Boaz was the man to whom everyone in the city looked as their leader. His exalted position enhances the humility and tenderness he shows as the story progresses. We should take note of his exalted position because as a Christ figure, he will rescue Ruth with humility and tender mercy. All of his might is directed not to his own glory but to the cause of the needy. As such, Boaz's mighty position enhances the ultimate humility that he shows to this needy widow. What a stunning picture of our Savior!

As the story unfolds, Samuel reveals Boaz's central importance as the kinsman-redeemer. This is yet another of the many literary devices that Samuel uses to awaken the reader's curiosity as well as to foreshadow what will happen next in the story. The story is structured to force us to think about what God will do for the future of this dead family. The literary structure drives us to ask, "Who is this man that we have just met, and what will he do in our story?" This means that as we read the story, we are driven to the future of this story, not only for what it means for our characters but also for us. Indeed, this is what one might describe as an eschatological quality to the whole story. The reader is required to ask, "Who are these people, and how do they relate to the overall story of the gospel?"

Samuel places Boaz in the first and last verse of this chapter, and he is clearly the pivotal character. He will mediate the "death to life" situation of our widows. He will act as the ultimate mediator. His description as a mighty man is not incidental to our story but directs us to calculate his vital role in the unfolding drama.

---

3   The word *eschatological* is connected not merely to "end times" but also to the future blessings of a new age.

It is helpful to notice that Boaz is related to the first men in our story but *by way of extreme contrast*. For instance, we can't help but juxtapose this new, strong man of chapter 2 with the weak man of chapter 1. So far, all the men introduced at the beginning of our story were weak and failing. Now God brings a strong man to the scene. Boaz will be the man who stands where the others have fallen. He is the one who remains strong and faithful. You can't miss Boaz's role as the savior of the story. He emerges on the scene and stands as the vital link between Ruth and Naomi. He rises as the connection between the death of their family and the hope of life. He becomes the link between the past and the future. Boaz holds, as it were, the destiny of these two widows in his hands.

Even though he is an old man, Boaz becomes associated with strength and hope. His name probably means "alacrity" (liveliness, alertness, action, willingness, readiness). He was an overcomer, a pillar. He foreshadows Jesus Christ and acts an example for those who would follow the Lord—Boaz is a pillar! We can see the theological connection of Boaz as a pillar in the temple of God in 1 Kings 7:21: "Then he set up the pillars by the vestibule of the temple; he set up the pillar on the right and called its name Jachin, and he set up the pillar on the left and called its name Boaz."

This gives us great insight as to what it means to be a pillar in the house of God. Boaz, who is a pillar in God's house, is like Christ, who is called the foundation stone of the house of God. And, like Christ, his mercy and strength is focused toward redeeming the needy. Boaz offers a sterling example of Christ's kindness as our Savior.

In 1 Kings 7:21 the origin of the name of the other pillar, Jachin, is unknown. We know nothing more of Jachin than that he was a pillar of faith. He was a great man of faith, and was so great that he was named a pillar in the house of

God. It is as if God has given us Boaz as a type of Christ, and then this unknown name points to the rest of us who follow in the way of Boaz or Christ. All the faithful of Christ become the pillars of the new temple, the church of Jesus Christ. Maybe you are a Jachin. Certainly Ruth's story highlights the extraordinary role that ordinary but faithful people play in the history redemption. According to Revelation 3:12, "He who overcomes, I will make him a pillar in the temple of My God, and he shall go out no more. And I will write on him the name of My God and the name of the city of My God, the New Jerusalem, which comes down out of heaven from My God. And I will write on him My new name."

Furthermore, those of us who long to be pillars in the house of God would do well to study the life of Boaz.[4] It looks as if Samuel is highlighting the life of Boaz to help us to understand the life of our blessed Savior, Jesus the Christ, and to amplify our understanding of godly character.

From the Fields of Moab to the Fields of Boaz

Ruth turns to the field of Boaz, which becomes the setting for the family's salvation. In a sense, there was actually only one field in the land. The fields of Israel were divided into plots of land for the various families. If you remember from the beginning of the tribal settlements, all the families were given plots of land, which belonged to them permanently. If they sold their fields, as Elimelech had done, they either had to wait for the Year of Jubilee or they had to rely on a kinsmen redeemer to buy back their land for them.

Ruth 1:1 stated that a certain man went to sojourn in the "fields" of Moab. Verse 2 says that the family entered the "fields" of Moab and remained there. Ruth 1:6 mentions that Naomi wanted to return from the fields of Moab, for

---

4   Jim Jordan, "Ruth."

she heard in the field of Moab that the Lord had visited
his people by giving them bread. Finally, in the last verse
of chapter 1, Samuel says they "returned from the fields of
Moab." This sets the stage for a contrast with the fields of
Bethlehem in Judah. It is helpful in terms of the theology of
the story to take note of the kinds of parallels or contrasts
that Samuel uses.

The story takes us from death in the fields of Moab to
the life in Boaz's portion of the fields of Judah. Ruth has
now left the *fields of Moab,* and she has taken refuge in the
fields of Boaz in Bethlehem of Judah. She has left the land
of her pagan forefathers, and she has now entered into the
Land of Promise. She is taking refuge in the land of God's
people. She leaves the fields of barrenness and death and
joins herself with the fields of harvest and life.

Laws of Gleaning

Since it was the harvest, it was an opportunity for those
who were being blessed to help those who were less
fortunate. Samuel provides us with yet another setting that
has powerful literary and theological meaning. It helps us to
make sense of the gleaning laws that played a central role in
the setting of our story.

We might be tempted to ask the question, "Why didn't
Boaz provide for Naomi and Ruth immediately when they
entered the city?" After all, he certainly had enough wealth
to help them out of their situation financially. Perhaps
he had questions about Naomi. After all, what kind of a
family leaves the land of Judah for Moab? Wasn't Naomi a
bitter old woman whose bitterness could poison the people
of God? God gave gleaning laws to help men ferret out
precisely these kinds of questions about a person's character.

The gleaning laws were helpful for people in all the
right ways. Gleaning, as we will see, was hardly a welfare
handout program. People who gleaned were not "on the

dole." God required the poor who were able-bodied to work for what they gleaned—they had to work very hard for the help that they received.

The fields were not shared in common in some kind of a socialistic manner. Rather, each family owned and cultivated its field or plot of ground. Hence, in Ruth 2:7, Samuel tells us that Ruth asked permission to glean. Perhaps in order to guard against the abuse of gleaning laws, the owners were at least notified. This would have been a practical and necessary growth of the practice of gleaning. In fact, it would be important to ensure that only the truly needy gleaned from the property. True generosity always distinguishes between the "worthy" poor and others. This may sound callous and contrary to charitable kindness, but it appears to be a necessary part of responsible charity. There is no doubt that Paul makes similar distinctions in 1 Timothy 5 when he speaks of widows who are worthy of the support of the church. God's love to the needy requires personal responsibility, which ultimately blesses those who give and those who receive.

The poor of the land were to be assisted. But most of them were helped as they were allowed to help themselves to the excess of the wealthy—they were *required to work*. God provided that the corners of fields were not to be reaped, and if you accidentally dropped a sheaf, you were required to leave it behind for the needy according to the law of Moses. Extra blessings were to be left for the poor to glean. Similar laws were given regarding vineyards and olive yards. Note Leviticus 19:9–10:

> When you reap the harvest of your land, you shall not wholly reap the corners of your field, nor shall you gather the gleanings of your harvest. And you shall not glean your vineyard, nor shall you gather every grape of your vineyard; you shall leave them for the poor and the stranger: I am the

LORD your God.

And Deuteronomy 24:19–22,

> When you reap your harvest in your field, and forget a sheaf
> in the field, you shall not go back to get it; it shall be for the
> stranger, the fatherless, and the widow, that the LORD your
> God may bless you in all the work of your hands. When
> you beat your olive trees, you shall not go over the boughs
> again; it shall be for the stranger, the fatherless, and the
> widow. When you gather the grapes of your vineyard, you
> shall not glean it afterward; it shall be for the stranger, the
> fatherless, and the widow. And you shall remember that you
> were a slave in the land of Egypt; therefore I command you
> to do this thing.

Gleanings are those pieces of barley or wheat that were
either not gathered or that had fallen to the ground in
the process of harvesting. These laws were perfect for the
rich and for the poor—they required the wealthy to have
a proper sensitivity to God's blessings and to those less
fortunate. They also required the poor to be responsible to
work, and to be accountable to property owners as well as
thankful for the blessings they received. God's people were
not to obsess with collecting every drop of God's riches.
Those who were blessed at harvest were required to share,
and those who were needy could not demand a handout—
they had to work. Those who had abundance were to
possess it with open hands. They were never allowed to
grasp too tightly to the material things with which God has
blessed them.

God's people are all beggars and suppliants; we are all
needy without the mercy of the Lord. God's people should
be so aware of the compassion that has been poured out
upon them that when they see the needy, they are reminded
of their own lot without God, and it should help them to
respond with God's compassion to others. God's people

(with Boaz as a classic example) ought to be characterized by kindness and mercy.

Widows

Ruth's story does not involve a needy widow as some kind of a massive coincidence. No, Ruth's story has covenant or theological purpose to it. Ruth was by all accounts a needy person in the land. She most certainly qualified as a needy person at virtually every level. She was a widow and a foreigner, which means that she was exposed and without security. Ruth needed a protector; she needed a savior.

Widows were to be treated with kindness (Ex. 22:22; Deut. 14:29; 16:11; 24:17–21; 26:12; 27:19). In the New Testament the same tender regard for them is inculcated (Acts 6:1–6; 1 Tim. 5:3–16) and exhibited. See also James 1:27: "Pure and undefiled religion before God and the Father is this: to visit orphans and widows in their trouble, and to keep oneself unspotted from the world."

The Beauty of Redemption: God the Poet, We His Poems

> Then she left, and went and gleaned in the field after the reapers. And she happened to come to the part of the field belonging to Boaz, who was of the family of Elimelech (2:3).

Samuel's deliberate use of the phrase "happened upon" the field of Boaz actually heightens our sense of the sovereign hand of God. God is crafting a masterpiece of redemption. With better dexterity than a Renaissance artist, God has been at work for many years. Indeed, the man Boaz is so beautifully created to be the absolutely perfect man to redeem Ruth that it should amaze us and inspire us.

It is good to reflect on the sovereign, artistic hand of God at work here in our story. God is the ultimate story teller and artist—he is the great poet of redemption. He not only creates the plot for the narrative, but he also sovereignly crafts everything in all of history towards the perfect

ending. Paul describes all Christians as the "poetry of God."
He says in Ephesians 2:10, "For we are His workmanship,
created in Christ Jesus for good works, which God prepared
beforehand that we should walk in them."

We ought to meditate on the love, the attention, the care,
the artistry that God gives to us. Here again we should be
moved by that reality as we consider the work of God in
our story. Of course Ruth did not just "happen" to walk
up to the fields of Boaz. Think of the beautiful irony in the
story so far. Elimelech didn't "happen" to fumble his way to
Moab from Bethlehem. The ironic reversal is unmistakable.
Did a man and woman whose names meant "God is my
king" and "pleasantness" really just happen to make the
choices that led them to have two sons named "weakness"
and "wasting away"?

The reversal of the curse of Moab through Ruth was not
a miracle of fate. What about the incestuous beginnings of
Moab as the source of the reversal of the incestuous break
in the tribe of Judah found in Genesis 38 with Judah and
Tamar? What a masterpiece of redemption! We ought to
recall that Moab was the son of Lot from an incestuous
relationship with his daughter. What a perfectly horrible
source for hope! Maybe not; maybe this is a perfectly
wonderful source of salvation to highlight the masterful
God of grace. God uses everything that humanly speaking
is completely the opposite. In God's artistic love he
highlights the strokes of an artist's brush as he reverses the
irreversible! No wonder one of the most popular hymns in
history is entitled "Amazing Grace."

As we read, we become blissfully aware that God had
been at work in this man, Boaz, just as God had been
at work with Ruth. Boaz is suited in so many ironic and
artistic ways to be the perfect man for Ruth. If we follow
the tidbits of information about Boaz in other sections
of the Bible, then we should be amazed. For instance, in

Matthew 1:5–6 we find recorded that Boaz was the son of Rahab the harlot: "Salmon begot Boaz by Rahab, Boaz begot Obed by Ruth, Obed begot Jesse, and Jesse begot David the king." Think of it! Who would be better fitted to appreciate our heroine Ruth than a man whose own mother had walked in Ruth's sandals? Yes, Rahab the harlot was Boaz's mother. Could there be a better man for Ruth?

Boaz of all men knew of the plight of strangers in the land, and he didn't know this plight from the Scriptures only. Because his mother, Rahab, had walked where Ruth was now walking, Boaz intimately understood the pain of being an alien woman in the land of Israel. He knew what it meant to need the mercy of the people of God. He had learned from his own mother to have a heart of mercy and kindness to the needy. He already knew what James would write centuries later when he said that true religion consists in looking after the orphan and widow in distress. What a poignant scene we have—Ruth the Moabitess meets the tenderhearted son of a former prostitute who had also been a foreigner in the land. What a beautiful story!

Here again Boaz points us to Jesus. Could there be a better Savior for us but Jesus? Jesus is the one who left heavenly glory to become a human like us. Jesus understands us. When we come to Him, we are coming to one who is not a distant judge or remote king, but we come to one who has himself been tested just as we are, yet without sin. Hebrews 4:14–16 says, "Seeing then that we have a great High Priest who has passed through the heavens, Jesus the Son of God, let us hold fast our confession. For we do not have a High Priest who cannot sympathize with our weaknesses, but was in all points tempted as we are, yet without sin. Let us therefore come boldly to the throne of grace, that we may obtain mercy and find grace to help in time of need."

God, the artist of redemption, God, the poet of salvation,

creates a masterpiece in everyone who believes. Who could remain silent in the presence of such amazing grace!

Questions for Consideration
1. Explain why the popular portrait of Ruth is wrong.
2. What is the theological significance of the "harvest"?
3. What does the title "mighty man of valor" mean?
4. How does this title highlight Boaz's acts of kindness?
5. What can we learn from this?
6. What is the significance of the setting in "fields"?
7. Describe the laws of gleaning.
8. Explain the artistry in God using Boaz.
9. How is there always similar artistry in our own salvation?

Lesson 8

The Response of the Humble

Ruth 2:4–14

The Encounter

The apex and center of chapter 2 is the God-ordained encounter of Ruth and Boaz. Samuel designed their meeting to be dramatic, and he uses the dialogue, the structure, and virtually everything in the whole story to pull us closer and closer to the center of the chapter, where the hero meets the heroine.

Samuel almost toys with us, indicating on the one hand that Ruth just "happened" to be in the right place at the right time, and "behold" Boaz arrived from Bethlehem. He heightens the providential sense of the story, saying that Ruth "happened" to be in the fields of Boaz. More literally the text says, "Her chance chanced upon." Well as "chance" would have it, behold, Boaz also went out into the field and addressed the gleaners.

Not only does Samuel accent their meeting with these kinds of statements but he also uses the structure of the story to move us towards their encounter. The story takes a dramatic turn from Ruth's journey up to this meeting in the field. Suddenly Samuel turns the eyes of everyone in the story to Boaz. Boaz enters with the dramatic word, "Behold." This is not the most common introduction of a character, and it is intended to create an almost theatrical flair to his entrance. One scholar notes that this word brings a touch of vividness to the narrative.[1] Indeed, we

---

1   Cundall & Morris, *Judges & Ruth*, 271.

don't have Boaz simply walking to his field, but it is more like an official "appearance" or a "coming." Behold, Boaz has come!

Samuel's description of Boaz as "coming" from Bethlehem adds another element of divine planning. Another scholar comments that the word "behold" expresses wonder at this arrival and its timing.[2] The savior of our story has arrived from Bethlehem. As the savior from Bethlehem arrives, he showers the workers with blessings. His first words are those of blessing. As he arrives, Boaz says to the harvesters, "The Lord be with you all." And they said, "The Lord bless you."

Boaz greets them with a traditional blessing/greeting. In fact, this is the same greeting traditionally used in the liturgy of western and eastern churches. In such instances the minister usually greets or addresses the congregation saying, "The Lord be with you," and the people respond saying, "And also with you."

Not only does Boaz bless them verbally, but he immediately engages in pastoral oversight. He is a pious and godly man in every way, and he immediately begins to watch over the harvest. One author says of Boaz, "An atmosphere of holiness pervades his person and everything around him, which will show itself repeatedly in the verses that follow."[3]

Like our Savior Jesus, Boaz does not randomly spread good tidings in some kind of a broad or indiscriminate way. Rather, he directs his specific kindness personally to Ruth. For instance, Boaz immediately recognized that there was a new gleaner. He recognized her and began to inquire

---

2   Daniel I. Block, *The New American Commentary, vol. 6, Judges, Ruth: An Exegetical and Theological Exposition of Holy Scripture* (Nashville: Broadman & Holman, 1999), 655.

3   LaCocque, *Ruth: A Continental Commentary*, 65.

about her. Samuel reminds us that Boaz met her because she "happened" to be in the tent taking a rest. She was providentially placed right in front of him.

> So the servant who was in charge of the reapers answered and said, "It is the young Moabite woman who came back with Naomi from the country of Moab. And she said, 'Please let me glean and gather after the reapers among the sheaves.' So she came and has continued from morning until now, though she rested a little in the house" (Ruth 2:6–7).

The man in charge had already granted Ruth permission to glean, and Boaz responded. He moved to her and addressed her directly:

> "You will listen, my daughter, will you not? Do not go to glean in another field, nor go from here, but stay close by my young women. Let your eyes be on the field which they reap, and go after them. Have I not commanded the young men not to touch you? And when you are thirsty, go to the vessels and drink from what the young men have drawn" (Ruth 2:8–9).

Imagine Ruth's overwhelming relief! She had been abandoned in the death of her husband, and she had left her homeland in pursuit of precisely this kind of covenant care from the Lord; now she has found it—better yet God has found her.

Boaz intended to supply all of her needs. He pledged that he would provide for her welfare from his own fields exclusively. He recognized that she was no mere gleaner; she was a member of his household, and he acknowledged that he would gladly take her as his personal responsibility.

Boaz specifically told his harvesters to allow Ruth to glean closely without any harassment. It appears that the gleaners would follow from a distance because the reapers didn't want them too close. Apparently the reapers would swat them back so that they would not interfere or so that they were not allowed into the unharvested grains.

Boaz told her that the servants have been commanded not to touch her. She may have faced the danger of rape or abuse. This would very likely be the case for an unprotected widow, but this would particularly be the case because she is a foreigner and, worse yet, she is a Moabitess. To whom would she go if someone were to take advantage of her? It isn't likely that Boaz would have workers of this sort. Still, it is possible. Boaz wanted her to have the special privilege of gleaning close to the reapers without being waved back or harmed. Ruth has found a refuge under the wings of a redeemer.

Boaz gave her a status above the normal gleaner. She was elevated in her needy estate to that of blessed estate. She became someone with Boaz's personal protection. For instance, she was given permission to drink from the water jar. No gleaner would have been allowed to do this. Water was the blessing of the owners and the workers who were harvesting. The gleaners would have had to provide for themselves. Therefore, when he gave her water, he elevated her to a privileged status. He was acting as a true king in Israel. Boaz had a heart for the needy, and he responded instinctively to his responsibilities as a kinsman-redeemer— he helped his family with a tender heart.

Boaz illustrates what a true king in Israel would be like, what a true husband would do. The true husband provides for his household. He pledges to be the sole provider of his household. What a great comfort to hear his words! What a warm encouragement to know that no one else will need to provide for your needs while you are in his household. There would be no need to look to anyone else for your welfare. Yes, just as Christ provides us with living water, so Boaz gave Ruth water to quench her thirst. Ruth will be the bride of the covenant, and Boaz will provide for her welfare. Boaz noted his reasons:

And Boaz answered and said to her, "It has been fully
reported to me, all that you have done for your mother-in-
law since the death of your husband, and how you have left
your father and your mother and the land of your birth, and
have come to a people whom you did not know before. The
LORD repay your work, and a full reward be given you by
the LORD God of Israel, under whose wings you have come
for refuge" (vv. 11–12).

Unlike the popular made-for-television versions of this
story, Boaz did not tell her that he loved her and wanted
her because she was so good looking. Some versions of this
story indicate that this was some kind of love at first sight
nonsense. Boaz was not struck by the beauty of her body
but by the beauty of her character. In fact, the age difference
seems to tell us that for Boaz, this was more of a fatherly
concern. Ruth was probably around twenty to twenty-five
years old, while Boaz was from Naomi's generation and
thus much older than Ruth.

We know this because he referred to Ruth as "daughter."
Remember, Boaz was a relative of Elimelech, and his initial
duty was to Naomi. Consequently, the age difference
between Ruth and Boaz would be roughly the same as
that between Ruth and Naomi. In fact, later in the story
he thanks her for her concern for him because of the vast
age difference: "Blessed are you of the LORD, my daughter!
For you have shown more kindness at the end than at the
beginning, in that you did not go after young men, whether
poor or rich" (3:10).

While it turns out to be a stunning love story, Samuel
makes it clear that Boaz's initial concerns originated from
godly intentions. Boaz intended to care for his obligations
as kinsman, and Ruth sought a godly solution to her woes.
Therefore, it appears from everything in the story that Boaz
had no romantic intentions when he helped her as he did.
This is not, therefore, a romance story. Boaz, as a man of

honor, took care of Ruth for Naomi's sake, and romance is not the focus of the scene. He showed her pity as someone with a responsible, tender heart. Likewise, as will be clear to us as the story unfolds, Boaz had nothing personally to gain from pursuing Ruth.

He was moved to a warm regard for her because she left her people and identified with God's people. She left her homeland to follow after the Lord. Aren't all of us moved deeply by a good conversion story? Certainly, Boaz was moved deeply by this young woman who followed in so many ways after the path of his own mother, Rahab. Boaz surely had Moses' song in Deuteronomy 32:11 in mind as the backdrop to his statement in Ruth 2:12 that Ruth had come to be sheltered under the wings of God.[4] This is also a helpful key for how we see this story. It is much more than a love story; it is the gospel story.

The gleaning process had revealed Ruth's true character; she was a woman of God. Indeed, as a woman of humility, she was constantly revealing her true humility when she responded to Boaz:

> Then she said, "Let me find favor in your sight, my lord; for you have comforted me, and have spoken kindly to your maidservant, though I am not like one of your maidservants" (Ruth 2:13).

Bread and Wine

> Now Boaz said to her at mealtime, "Come here, and eat of the bread, and dip your piece of bread in the vinegar." So she sat beside the reapers, and he passed parched grain to her; and she ate and was satisfied, and kept some back (Ruth 2:14).

---

4 David Atkinson develops this theme insightfully in his book, *The Wings of Refuge: The Message of Ruth*. See especially pp. 75–77.

In this scene, Boaz tells her to draw near. He served her and cared for her, providing her with bread and wine. Thus Boaz invited her to a covenant meal, making her a member of his household.

You don't need to look very far in the Scriptures to see that eating a meal signifies far more than just filling the stomach. Indeed, at Sinai in Exodus 24 we see that the elders of the nation of Israel went part of the way up the mountain and sat down with Moses and Aaron and shared a meal in the presence of God:

> Then he took the Book of the Covenant and read in the hearing of the people. And they said, "All that the LORD has said we will do, and be obedient." And Moses took the blood, sprinkled it on the people, and said, "This is the blood of the covenant which the LORD has made with you according to all these words." Then Moses went up, also Aaron, Nadab, and Abihu, and seventy of the elders of Israel, and they saw the God of Israel. And there was under His feet as it were a paved work of sapphire stone, and it was like the very heavens in its clarity. But on the nobles of the children of Israel He did not lay His hand. So they saw God, and they ate and drank (Ex. 24:7–11).

The word of God is full of festivals and meals to which the Lord invites us to come to enjoy him and his love. Heaven is even described as a great wedding feast of celebration where God's people celebrate the overwhelming grace of God.

Sharing a meal was genuinely covenantal. The host gave symbolically to the guest and thus shared life with them. When God shares a meal with us, he shares himself with us. This is a helpful point to remember when we have the Lord's Supper. There is something powerfully symbolic when God shares a meal with us.

This is true of times in redemptive history when servants or outcasts are invited to share a meal with someone who rescues or saves them. In some cases covenant meals indicated that the servant who was receiving mercy was by means of the meal being elevated to the status of a member of the household. There is a great example of this in the beautiful meal to which David invited Mephibosheth:

> So David said to him, "Do not fear, for I will surely show you kindness for Jonathan your father's sake, and will restore to you all the land of Saul your grandfather; and you shall eat bread at my table continually." Then he bowed himself, and said, "What is your servant, that you should look upon such a dead dog as I?" . . . So Mephibosheth dwelt in Jerusalem, for he ate continually at the king's table (2 Sam. 9:7–8, 13).

In this sense it looks like Boaz symbolically invited Ruth to join his household as she eats with them. Furthermore, he was the one who served her. Where it says he "served her roasted grain," it literally means "he heaped up the portion of her food." He gave more than enough for her to eat. He gave her bread and wine and fed her abundantly. She is served so much that she takes leftovers back home to Naomi. As David rescued Mephibosheth, so Boaz rescues Ruth. The picture is too beautiful to miss. Boaz does for Ruth what Jesus does for all of His humble followers—Boaz is typological of Jesus.

Ruth has unique permission to glean anything that has fallen down from among Boaz's personal harvest. These sheaves were the bundled piles or stands of harvested foods. The gleaners were not allowed to partake of the sheaves, because the sheaves were actually part of the harvest. This is a special provision of mercy that comes from his storehouse. He even told his men purposefully to leave some out for Ruth among the sheaves. Ruth is getting Boaz's own personal harvest.

She had separated the kernels from the husks, the chaff and the stalks, and she still had a huge amount left over.

Because of Boaz's generosity, Ruth was able to glean so much that she had an *ephah* of barley. Scholars note that an *ephah* was about a half bushel of barley. This is such a large amount that when Naomi saw it, she was amazed. Not only did Ruth bring home an amazing amount of barley, but she brought her mother-in-law the meal from lunch.

Naomi pronounces a blessing. It appears that she was saying, "May that man be blessed of the Lord, and the Lord has not withdrawn his kindness to the living and the dead." This appears to be the beginning of Naomi's repentance and confession. God has dealt kindly with her. Naomi is now becoming pleasant again. Naomi was gently restored from bitterness to joy in the covenant. Naomi says to Ruth in 2:22, "It is good, my daughter, that you go out with his young women, and that people do not meet you in any other field."

Finally Naomi is giving someone good advice! Salvation is coming, and it appears that even Naomi has started to recognize that the hope of the covenant really does come to those who seek it by faith. Naomi finally begins to direct Ruth to safety, hope and protection.

A likely interpretation of Naomi's advice is that she wanted Ruth to show Boaz that she trusted in his protection. If she went into other fields, the girls of Boaz might see her, and Boaz might think that she did not really trust him. It was important that she put her trust in Boaz. Naomi seems to indicate that since Boaz has taken care of Ruth, she should not look anywhere else for help. This is the way we also should look for help. Our help is in the Lord. This is why we humbly pray, "Give us this day our daily bread." We are to look to Christ alone for help and life.

Ruth's Reaction

Ruth responded to Boaz as a humble suppliant. She was overwhelmed with Boaz's kindness, and she responded properly as a humble receiver of grace and mercy. She did not deserve the mercy she gained, but she had been blessed, and she recognized this with humility.

This is exactly the humility that Ruth had already displayed. Her humility led her here. Indeed, earlier she indicated that she already understood her humble lot as a foreign widow. She had told Naomi in Ruth 2:2, "Please let me go to the field, and glean heads of grain after him *in whose sight I may find favor.*" Ruth used a phrase that is quite revealing. It clearly suggests her demeanor as a humble woman of God. She used a phrase that had originally served as a formula in the royal courts. It was used of subordinates who are addressing a ruler in whose presence they don't believe themselves to be equal. Consider the response of the Egyptians to Joseph when he provided for them during the famine: "So they said, 'You have saved our lives; let us find favor in the sight of my lord, and we will be Pharaoh's servants'" (Gen. 47:25). The phrase expressed more than simple courtesy. It communicated a true sense of dependence on someone else who was recognized as superior and capable of providing for one's needs. Ruth recognized her position and her need of someone who would give her grace.

The scene, like that of a royal court, presents us also with the need of the king or redeemer to look upon her with favor. If the king, or in this case, Boaz, found the servant "in his eyes" to be acceptable, he could choose to provide for her. Perhaps you can recall Queen Esther's precarious position in approaching the great King Ahasuerus, who had already shown himself capable of treachery towards his own wife. That is, after all, how Esther had become queen. We can all recall the scene in which she approaches the

king: "So it was, when the king saw Queen Esther standing
in the court, that she found favor in his sight, and the king
held out to Esther the golden scepter that was in his hand.
Then Esther went near and touched the top of the scepter"
(Est. 5:2). The outsider is welcomed as an insider. The one
with no ethnic claim to protection under the wings of the
Lord is now assured of the very same protection as God's
people. Boaz assured Ruth that the Lord God would cover
her and be her refuge. Surely Boaz's heart was warmed to
see this poor young widow taking refuge under the wings of
the Lord, just as his mother had once done. Boaz was acting
in regard to his role as her protector—what a tender scene!

Salvation

As we read, we can hear the sound of salvation in the
echoes of this story. Listen again to the description. Ruth
fled to Boaz's fields, but only as she had fled to the Lord's
protection "under his wings." In our Lord's ministry among
the Israelites, he was constantly calling people to turn away
from former things so they could turn fully to him. One
way you hear this described is when Jesus says, "He who
loves father or mother more than Me is not worthy of Me.
And he who loves son or daughter more than Me is not
worthy of Me. And he who does not take his cross and
follow after Me is not worthy of Me. He who finds his life
will lose it, and he who loses his life for My sake will find
it" (Matt. 10:37–39).

This is clearly a redemptive theme. Why had Ruth left
Moab? She had nothing physically in Bethlehem; why
would she go there? Boaz tells us that Ruth had left her
father and mother in Moab, but what motivated her? It
was for faith in the Lord that she left. She fled to find
refuge under the wings of the Lord. When the reader keeps
redemption central to his understanding of this story, it
comes alive with deep meaning.

Ruth's Response

> So she fell on her face, bowed down to the ground, and said to him, "Why have I found favor in your eyes, that you should take notice of me, since I am a foreigner?" (Ruth 2:10).

How else could she respond? She has fled for refuge under the shadow of her new savior's wings. She has not only been helped but also elevated to join in a meal with her master. Isn't such singing and gratitude the only proper response? Wouldn't anyone in such a position cry out with an overwhelming sense of thanksgiving? God's grace has overwhelmed her, and she cries out appropriately.

There is salvation for all who will flee to the Savior for refuge. Does this not also penetrate our own hearts as we see our own condition before the great Kinsman-Redeemer? Don't forget, beloved Boaz has a son; Christ Jesus is the future son of Boaz, and he will redeem his bride in the same way. And likewise Ruth's response is the response of all those who have been taken under the shadow of his wings.

Will you join with Ruth in her appreciation of the grace of God? Come to the table of the Lord as she did, with a heart overawed by the grace of God through Jesus. Why, O Lord, would you love one such as I? Why, O Lord, would you take me under your wings for refuge? Ruth's story is our story! Will you join Ruth in her response?

Questions for Consideration

1. Describe some of the ways Samuel highlights the importance of Ruth meeting Boaz.
2. Describe how Boaz's love was pointed and personal.
3. What specific things did Boaz do to show this love?
4. In what way does he play the role of a husband?
5. Explain the importance of the phrase, "under the wings of God."

7. Why are meals important?
8. How did this meal symbolize Ruth's entry into a household?
9. What indicates that Naomi's heart was softening?
10. Describe Ruth's response, and explain why it should be our response.

Lesson 9

Redemption Assured

Ruth 3

The Final Turning Point

In chapter 2 Samuel gives the account of Boaz and Ruth's first meeting. In chapter 3 we discover the couple's second meeting, the most pivotal circumstance of the whole story. Like the meeting in chapter 2, this is not a mere chance encounter; this meeting is divinely arranged. The tension of this encounter is heightened because Ruth takes an extreme risk in approaching Boaz the way she does. One author notes, "Boaz could have taken advantage of Ruth's offer without risking any consequences even if she became pregnant by him. In short, Ruth places herself in extreme danger, so that if there was a trap on her part, as several commentators indicate, it will snap shut more surely on her than on Boaz."[1]

This is definitely the turning point of the story, and we draw this conclusion because of the structure Samuel uses. As in chapter 2, the central dialogue between Ruth and Boaz interrupts two other dialogues between Ruth and Naomi. Samuel consciously structures the story in a way to deepen what we are learning.

One scholar notes, "The Bible's value as a religious document is intimately and inseparably related to its value as literature."[2] Thus, we need to pay attention to such things as structure, style, and word use. As we have seen

---

1 André LaCocque, *Ruth*, 83.

2 Robert Alter, *The Art of Biblical Narrative*, 19.

already, Samuel uses a symmetrical, funnel-like structure that guides us to the central encounter between Boaz and Ruth. Everything is prearranged to converge at this point. The same kind of structure occurs in Ruth 2, except in Ruth 3 the stakes are quite high, and the drama brings the whole story to a point of climax and ultimate decision.

In chapter 2, for instance, in their first encounter, Boaz and Ruth meet in the field. The description of that meeting is flanked by two dialogues between Ruth and Naomi. Chapter 3 becomes the decisive encounter whereby God reverses Ruth's destiny. A series of ironic reversals occur in the story between our hero and heroine. These incidents reveal a definite connection between what happened at the beginning of the story and what God is doing to reverse the story. We see, for instance, that the chapters contain parallels that have necessary and significant developments. Notice the following parallel developments:

- From the fields to the threshing floor
- From public to private
- From day to night
- From chance to choice
- From Boaz active to Boaz passive
- From Ruth passive to Ruth active

These significant parallels and developments lead us inexorably to the redemption that is at the heart of the story. Indeed, the apex of this pattern is found in chapter 3 when Ruth approaches Boaz in the middle of the night. Ruth has set her path toward Boaz, and we are uncertain what will happen. Ruth willingly lays herself down at Boaz's feet, whereby she faithfully follows the Lord in seeking a redeemer. But what will happen? The tension is elevated because Boaz is startled and awakened abruptly. How will he respond, and what will he do?

Boaz tells Ruth not to be afraid, and he assures her that

he will care for her and care for his duty as her kinsman-redeemer. Boaz most certainly could have taken advantage of this vulnerable young woman. Instead, he is moved with love and compassion for her. Instead of taking advantage of her, he protects her. What a man! Ruth's initiative evokes a selfless tenderness in Boaz as he responds to her request. He compliments our heroine in the name of the Lord and recognizes the hand of God upon her.

Naomi's Request

> Then Naomi her mother-in-law said to her, "My daughter, shall I not seek security for you, that it may be well with you?" (Ruth 3:1).

Samuel describes Naomi as Ruth's mother-in-law, which seems to reflect her growing love for Ruth. Of course, we know already that Naomi is Ruth's mother-in-law, but here she is finally treating Ruth as if she were her own daughter. Naomi reveals her affection and love for Ruth as she begins to plan for her security and interests. If we pay careful attention to the story, we witness an ever-so-gentle change in Naomi. The Lord has softened her, and she is now doing for her daughter-in-law what she should have done when they were in Moab. Remember, this is the same Naomi who was at first urging both her daughters-in-law to return to their Moabite families. At that point in the story Naomi, whose name means "pleasant," was bitter; now Naomi has become pleasant again.

In fact, Naomi's request to provide security for Ruth indicates that she is acting by faith. Some may suggest that Naomi is acting with selfish regard for her own welfare, especially because of the potential danger in which she puts Ruth. I don't think this is the case. To the contrary, Naomi reveals faith that the *goel*, the kinsman-redeemer Boaz, will provide for Ruth. Though this was not the case at the beginning of the story, Naomi is now speaking on behalf of Ruth; she has Ruth's best interests at heart; she points her to the plan of God for precisely this kind of need.

Rest and Well-Being

Naomi believes that her daughter-in-law will find two things with Boaz—rest and well-being. *Rest* is something that is holistic in the Bible, and the concept of rest has richer and deeper meaning in the Old Testament than it does today. When someone says that he could use some rest, he generally is speaking of something physical. The Old Testament concept of rest is more pervasive and comprehensive than mere physical respite.

Rest in the Old Testament includes the idea of peace, security, and blessings. This is why we see Naomi saying that she will seek rest for Ruth. Notice that Naomi does believe that Ruth can find both rest and well-being in Boaz. For a woman in that culture, the concept of rest often included marriage and the security of a home. While this notion annoys some feminist critics who read this story, it nevertheless accords with creation design. The Bible speaks of marriage as including rest and well-being in covenant with God. The beautiful theme that keeps popping up in our story is the idea of being covered with protection and security.

Naomi is definitely playing matchmaker for her daughter-in-law. However, we soon discover that there is risk involved in this encounter with Boaz, and not merely the risk of meeting someone and being rejected. There is a much greater risk for Ruth, and the secrecy Naomi encourages Ruth to use demonstrates the nature of the risk.

This accounts for Ruth's approaching Boaz at night. Naomi tells Ruth not to show herself early. Rather, she is to wait until later, when everyone is asleep; she is to sneak in at dark. If she were caught in the area, she may have been required to leave, and she would have lost her opportunity. She was to observe the scene and then quietly uncover Boaz's feet. Here we are helped if we understand that the biblical phrase "uncovering the feet" means much more than merely taking off his sandals. It appears to be a euphemism for physical intimacy. Thus, Naomi told Ruth, "Therefore wash yourself and anoint yourself, put on your best garment and go down to the threshing floor" (3:3).

Naomi told Ruth to clean herself, put on her best clothes, and perfume herself—as a bride—for Boaz. She was to look as beautiful as possible.

> So she went down to the threshing floor and did according to all that her mother-in-law instructed her. And after Boaz had eaten and drunk, and his heart was cheerful, he went to lie down at the end of the heap of grain; and she came softly, uncovered his feet, and lay down (3:6–7).

The text literally says that it was well with him. This corresponds to Ruth 3:1: "My daughter, shall I not seek security for you, that it *may be well with you?*" (emphasis added). The phrase seems to be connected with this particular scene. In other words, if Ruth can join herself with Boaz, then it will be well with her also. It is well with Boaz, and he is the one who is able to provide well-being for Ruth. God makes it clear that she needs a husband, which is why Ruth has followed the will of God in approaching Boaz as her kinsman-redeemer rather than other men she could have approached. She is faithful here in so many ways commendable to women of faith.

Please note that Ruth is not modeling for us any kind of an approach to courtship or dating. For those of you who are always looking to the Bible for examples of how this or that practice should be followed, you might be surprised. I have found that many proponents of specific "models" of marriage and courtship look to the Bible to provide evidence for their specific practice. However, we should be cautious about using ancient practices as "the model" for our present activities, lest we conclude that a woman should be like Ruth and pursue a man she believes is good for her. Here, as in other cases in Scripture, the ancient practice is descriptive—not prescriptive.

The Threshing Floor

> "Now Boaz, whose young women you were with, is he not our relative? In fact, he is winnowing barley tonight at the threshing floor" (3:2).

Everything will be played out on the threshing floor, which plays a role in the setting of redemption and restoration. It presents a dramatic scene for the ultimate turning point of our story. Why would this be the setting? Does it have significance? We need to remember that the Bible's value as a religious document is intimately and inseparably related to its value as literature.[3]

Consequently, it is natural for us to look for literary clues in the story and to understand that the threshing floor is a metaphor with definite theological connotations. It is the place of judgment; it is the place of ultimate separation. Here is where the wheat is beaten from the chaff. The threshing floor is where the good is separated from the bad, and thus the landscape is significant for the story. This is the moment of truth. LaCoque observes, "Naomi was possibly sending her daughter-in-law to her destruction—or at least to the confirmation for witnesses that one can expect nothing more than promiscuity from Moab. Ruth was perhaps going to be mistaken for a prostitute. Boaz was perhaps going to commit irreparable harm."

Boaz and his men are enjoying a celebration on the threshing floor at the end of harvest. This could have been

---

3   Robert Alter, *The Art of Biblical Narrative*.

some kind of a threshing party for all the men. The place where the gathering was held could have been a threshing station of some sort. Perhaps different harvesting groups used the floor at different times, and this must have been Boaz's night at the threshing floor. At any rate, Boaz was not alone. We know this because Naomi told Ruth to mark which spot was Boaz's when he lay down.

Perhaps this was the combination of a massive work day and then, as the day closed, a huge party to match the work. There was feasting and drinking. It appears that this Israelite celebration was unique among ancient Near East harvest festivals, in that it *did not include women.* The pagan harvest festivals commonly celebrated the gods of fertility, and orgies and perversions of all sorts occurred. Indeed, temple prostitutes were commonplace during these festivals. We should already know that harvesting and sheep shearing were used as opportunities for celebrations of excess. It is no small coincidence that the story harkens back to a fateful moment in Genesis 38 when Judah thought the presence of a temple prostitute a rather unremarkable reality for such celebrations. Women are not a part of Boaz's celebration.

> So she lay at his feet until morning, and she arose before one could recognize another. Then he said, "Do not let it be known that the woman came to the threshing floor" (3:14).

Midnight?

In considering the setting, we find yet another seemingly insignificant detail that points to the gravity of what happens at the threshing floor. Ruth's dramatic awakening of Boaz comes at midnight. Like the threshing floor, the time setting of midnight points to a dramatic time of judgment and decision. It marks a turning point. Midnight is the time of life and death in a handful of biblical narratives. From the earliest stages of redemptive history, midnight marks a time of dramatic decision. In the Scriptures as well, midnight marks the decisive moment of reckoning and redemption. Exodus 12:29–30 describes the most dramatic of these moments:

> And it came to pass at *midnight* that the LORD struck all the firstborn in the land of Egypt, from the firstborn of Pharaoh who sat on his throne to the firstborn of the captive who was in the dungeon, and all the firstborn of livestock. So Pharaoh rose in the night, he, all his servants, and all the Egyptians; and there was a great cry in Egypt, for there was not a house where there was not one dead (emphasis added).

Midnight became a fixed time of reckoning for the Old Testament saints, and it even became a time of prayer that marked the very pattern of their lives, as indicated in Psalm 119:62: "At *midnight* I will rise to give thanks to You, because of Your righteous judgments" (emphasis added).

Midnight came to be so commonly associated with judgment and reckoning that Jesus' New Testament parables often include this theme. For instance, the parable of the foolish virgins who run out of oil while they are waiting for the coming of the groom includes the midnight theme: "But while the bridegroom was delayed, they all slumbered and slept. And at *midnight* a cry was heard: 'Behold, the bridegroom is coming; go out to meet him!'" (Matt. 25:5–6, emphasis added).

Of course, in our story, midnight was the decisive moment as well. Rabbi Ginsburg notes:

> Its importance lies in the fact that it is linked to the future. Even though the night is the time of Hashem's strict justice and the morning is the time of mercy, from midnight on the time is influenced by the morning and is considered within the realm of mercy . . . Boaz arose that midnight to withstand the test of Ruth's presence, and this worked out in

the best manner as it was a time of mercy. [4]

Boaz lies down at the end of a heap of grain, sleeping next to his harvest. The whole harvest belongs to Boaz, and it looks like this great man can have whatever he wants. As he is sleeping, Ruth uncovers his feet, and he awakens: "Now it happened at midnight that the man was startled, and turned himself; and there, a woman was lying at his feet"(3:8).

Boaz was startled by the presence and activity of Ruth. Some scholars argue that she merely or literally uncovered his feet. However, it seems that more was going on here than this. "Uncovering his feet" appears to be a euphemism for attempting to take off his clothes. He was warm, and as he was uncovered, he awoke in surprise. Some commentators argue that Ruth did have relations with Boaz because of the use of this euphemism. This simply does not accord with Boaz's response of refusal. It is important to note that Boaz stops whatever potential relationship that could have occurred as a result of Ruth's activity.

Question of Identity

Because of the utter darkness, Boaz knew that the "intruder" was a woman but was startled at her presence and asked who she was. "So she answered, 'I am Ruth, your maidservant. Take your maidservant under your wing, for you are a close relative'" (3:9). This is the question that dominates the scene: Who are you? Boaz responds that he is in fact a close relative, and this is the word *goel*. The *goel* is the close relative obliged to redeem things on behalf of the family. Ruth appeals to Boaz, essentially asking him to respond to her needs, claiming him as her kinsman-redeemer. She begs Boaz to claim her as his wife.

The imagery of spreading a garment or skirt over someone

---

4 Ginsburg, *Mother of Kings*, 111.

is used to indicate marriage, and this is exemplified in
Ezekiel 16:7–9:

> "I made you thrive like a plant in the field; and you grew,
> matured, and became very beautiful. Your breasts were
> formed, your hair grew, but you were naked and bare. When
> I passed by you again and looked upon you, indeed your
> time was the time of love; so I spread My wing over you and
> [clothed] your nakedness. Yes, I swore an oath to you and
> entered into a covenant with you, and you became Mine,"
> says the Lord GOD.

The symbolism in this passage points to the covenant
made at Sinai. However, the analogy here is to the marriage
covenant. The marriage covenant is said to occur when
the husband covers his wife with his clothing. It is as if
they are now clothed with one cloth instead of two; they
become one. Since clothing relates to the glory and honor of
external appearance, they have one covering of glory
and honor. So in this incident, Ruth is inviting Boaz to
marry her.

It seems most likely that the earlier reference to Ruth's
uncovering Boaz's feet, a gesture of intimacy, is a reference
to her marriage invitation. Boaz was not being invited to
agree to some future ceremony; he was invited to marry
her on the spot. While in many cases in the ancient world
there were extravagant wedding celebrations, there was no
ceremony that matches the common Western notion of a
wedding. Rather, there was simply the consummation, and
this began the marriage. It appears that Ruth and Boaz
would not have needed any formal ceremony. The only
reason there is a legal exchange at the gate later in the story
is because there was another kinsman who had prior claims.

As there was no ceremony required, Boaz could easily
have taken advantage of Ruth's offering. Instead, he refused
to sin, and he resolved to love her. This was no easy thing,
my friends! Surely his heart raced and pounded as much

as any other man's would have as he saw and felt this beautiful young woman lying at his feet, offering herself to him. Boaz expresses his deepest affection for Ruth as he shows restraint and properly refuses to consummate their love. He was a man of godly honor, and God had touched his heart with deeply rooted integrity. Here is the man who walks in the path of the Lord.

> Then he said, "Blessed are you of the LORD, my daughter! For you have shown more kindness at the end than at the beginning, in that you did not go after young men, whether poor or rich (3:10).

Boaz is not expressing some kind of a romantic notion of love; his words are clear and covenantal. Boaz is referring to Ruth's actions in regard to Naomi. He remained completely in control of himself and focused the entire event on God and his covenant.

Boaz says, "For you have shown more kindness at the end than at the beginning." Boaz was referring to another act of kindness in keeping with Ruth's covenant obligations. The first act of covenant kindness was her choice to follow Naomi and become a member of God's covenant people. This included Ruth's hard work in gleaning for Naomi. Ruth did for Naomi what she could not do for herself, taking the place of an older widow. The second kindness is her offering herself as a substitute for Naomi. She did not have to do this. She was legally free to find herself another husband and did not have to perform the duty of a levirate. Instead, she acted on behalf of Naomi. Samuel presents us with two outstanding examples in Ruth and Boaz as they act on behalf of others.

Their covenant kindness is rewarded greatly. We often think that acting for others will yield endless toil with no reward. However, our heavenly rewards are far greater than the earthly rewards we forsake. There is so much in this

beautiful story about sacrifice and service for others. Ruth
could have found a man she wanted because he was young
and handsome. Yet she served her family without regard to
her own well-being. This is ironic, because in doing so, she
found the true source of well-being in Boaz.

Boaz, likewise, is not attracted to Ruth necessarily
because of her youth or outward beauty; he is attracted to
her covenant faithfulness. As a true husband and as a true
king in Israel, Boaz responds with covenant faithfulness
and points us to Ruth's interest in the covenant. She was
not interested in young men, either for emotional love or
for money; she was a woman of the covenant. Because of
this, Boaz agreed to marry her. However, he shows amazing
self-restraint and refrains from acting until he has notified
another man who has a closer claim than he has. Boaz acts
as a true and faithful husband.

He tells Ruth that he will do all that she asks of him. He
will marry her, and he will take care of her. He will raise
up a seed for Naomi and Elimelech. He will do everything
in his power to love Ruth and care for her. This man Boaz
was simply outstanding. Boaz is an admirable man. Every
dad wants a man like Boaz to marry or at least to date his
daughter. Every godly woman should be looking for this
man! Boaz is a type of Christ, like his predecessor Joseph.
Both are men who love when others would take advantage.

When we learn about men like Joseph and Boaz at their
best, we learn of our Savior. Notice what Boaz does. He
tells Ruth that he will follow the law because he knows
of another man whose covenantal/legal position is closer
than his. Therefore, he tells her to lie down at his feet until
morning. This phrase seems most certainly to be literal
rather than euphemistic. Ruth is to remain there and then
leave quietly at dawn. Boaz also restrains himself in regard
to loving her until he has fulfilled his obligations to God.

Boaz even protected Ruth from potential criticism.

He made sure that nobody thought improperly of her.
Boaz knew of the potential danger to her reputation as a
foreigner from the land of Moab, where there were temple
prostitutes who were commonly promiscuous during harvest
celebrations. Boaz sought to protect her. He encouraged her
to leave and gave her six measures of barley. It appears that
Boaz gives her something that will provide an explanation if
she is questioned. But certainly also it is a gift and token of
his love.

Question of Identity

> And she came in unto her mother-in-law, and she said, 'Who
> [are] you, my daughter?' and she declared to her all that the
> man had done to her (3:16, emphasis added).

Naomi asks Ruth who she is. This reminds of us Boaz's
earlier question, but Naomi was essentially asking Ruth if
she had gotten married. In other words, Naomi is asking
Ruth if she now is Mrs. Boaz. In this scene, Ruth now has
the identity of an Israelite, and there is also the obvious
and uncontrollable excitement that Naomi would have
experienced as Ruth returned from such an adventure.
We can only imagine the two of them jumping up and
down and hugging as Ruth shared with Naomi what had
happened. Imagine these two women as they laughed, cried,
and talked about the night's amazing encounter with a
genuine man of God.

Chapter 3 includes the themes of rest, security, peace, and
comfort. Boaz is going to provide all of these things for
Ruth through his legal work as the true husband. As Boaz
performs his legal duty, he provides rest for his bride. Ruth
depends entirely on Boaz for any hope of rest, and this is
certainly a picture of what Christ does for us.

The Reversal and Beauty of Grace:

There is much in the Bible about the love between a

husband and a wife. Our story of Ruth and Boaz moves us emotionally to imagine the tenderness, the gentleness, and the passion of Boaz and Ruth. Yet this grand love story isn't merely about a man and a woman but also about Christ and his bride, the church.

The more we meditate on Boaz's love for Ruth, the more overwhelmed we should become. This is the love of a faithful kinsman-redeemer. He is not looking for what he can get from this young woman; on the contrary, he covers her in ways that are not selfish. His love is unselfish and deep. This is the kind of love that provokes a wife to warm responsiveness.

This is godly, marital love. This is not mere romance, but it is a love deeply rooted in the vows and commitments that comprise a wedding ceremony. "I vow to love you for better or for worse, in sickness and in health, in plenty and in want, for richer or poorer." As these vows are tested and tried in the midst of the hardships of life, a deep love develops—a love that is so profound that only the word *mystery* can capture something of its character. This is not the frothy, romantic love we hear about in pop songs on our radios; this is true, sacrificial love that points us to Jesus. This is the love that drives us to our knees in wonder before our compassionate God.

Questions for Consideration
1. Describe the ironic reversals so far in the story.
2. What was Naomi's request, and how does it point to a change in her heart?
3. What is the significance of the threshing floor and of midnight?
4. Why was Ruth's request essentially a proposal of marriage?
5. Explain the symbolism in this part of the story.

6. Describe Boaz's response to Ruth's request for marriage.
7. Why does Naomi's question of identity further prove that marriage was the focus?
8. How is Boaz a type of Christ?
9. When you think of Boaz's love, is this the way you think of God's love and grace to you?

The Levirate Laws

The book of Ruth is one of the few places in the Bible where the levirate laws find their fullest expression. In fact, we can see the levirate laws in action throughout the whole story. Yet, because Ruth's story has so many interesting twists and turns, we really need to view her story in light of the levirate laws as they were first given in Deuteronomy. From this vantage point, we should be able to understand Ruth with richer insight.

What are these strange arrangements called levirate laws? In some ways they provide for one of the most bizarre arrangements in the whole Bible. They are also one of the keys for unlocking and appreciating the story of Ruth with the greatest depth. In Jewish circles the practice prescribed in the levirate laws is known as *yibbum*. The more commonly known name *levirate* comes from the Latin, *levir,* which means "a husband's brother." Though the words sound similar, the levirate laws do not have anything to do with Levi, the tribe given priestly authority in the land. The levirate laws involve an ancient custom observed by the patriarchs and officially ordained by Moses in Deuteronomy 25:5–10:

> If brothers *dwell together,* and one of them dies and has no son, the widow of the dead man shall not be married to a stranger outside the family; her husband's brother shall go in to her, take her as his wife, and perform the duty of a husband's brother to her. And it shall be that the firstborn son which she bears will succeed to the name of his dead

brother, *that his name may not be blotted out* of Israel. But if the man does not want to take his brother's wife, then let his brother's wife go up to the gate to the elders, and say, "My husband's brother refuses to raise up a name to his brother in Israel; he will not perform the duty of my husband's brother." Then the elders of his city shall call him and speak to him. But if he stands firm and says, "I do not want to take her," then his brother's wife shall come to him in the presence of the elders, remove his sandal from his foot, spit in his face, and answer and say, "So shall it be done to the man who will not build up his brother's house." And his name shall be called in Israel, "The house of him who had his sandal removed" (emphasis added).

This is the explanation: If an Israelite died without a child for his inheritance, then his brother was required to marry the widow in order to keep the deceased brother's name alive. The firstborn son of their union would inherit the deceased brother's name and land. The objective was "to resurrect or to raise up children on behalf of the dead brother." This is why their firstborn son would take the name and inheritance of his dead "father" instead of his biological father.

This is definitely one of those strange areas of Old Testament law, and it's natural to wonder about its purpose. The first stipulation seems to indicate that the *brothers live together.* This would mean that the brothers would be somewhat close in age. This would also seem to imply that the brothers knew their obligations, and they might very well have been involved in the choice of the wife in the first place.

Certainly if a younger brother knew that he may be required to marry his older brother's wife, he would be motivated to see his brother make a wise choice. One can imagine that in this context a family would take care to ensure that their son's wife was not a shrew. We may also assume that the younger brother might be expected to acknowledge the union in some way, perhaps requiring some kind of an agreement in the marriage. In today's culture, few of us have much to say when our sibling chooses a spouse. However, if we knew that we might be required to marry our sibling's spouse, we would probably be much more attentive to his or her choice. We can find the levirate laws in action in Genesis 38 in the account of Judah and Tamar. Here we see that the whole family, including the father, was on some level expected to support the levirate institution. Genesis 38 is not only important as a story involving the levirate laws, but it is also directly related to the story of Ruth.

The Duty
From Genesis 38 it becomes clear that a younger brother does not have the legitimate option of ignoring his responsibilities. He must perform his obligations to God and to his family, or he must face humiliating consequences. We also learn in this story that the obligations extend outward from the immediate younger brother to the next in line as it relates to the family's inheritance. Indeed, if there are no more younger brothers, then the duty extends outward from the immediate family, but there are fewer consequences for someone not in the immediate family who refuses to act as a levir. In other words, it appears that there is an option for more distant relatives, and duty is limited to the immediate family.

It is this distant relative's option that Boaz exercises in the book of Ruth. Boaz did not have a direct duty as the younger brother, which demonstrates that Boaz exercised his option out of love. In Deuteronomy 25, if the younger brother refuses to do his duty, he is publicly humiliated. His sandal is publicly removed, and the woman spits in his face. In Ruth, we see that this consequence does not exist for distant relatives; there is no shame for the distant relative who refuses to exercise his option. This fact accentuates the selfless quality of Boaz's love for Ruth.

He Married Her

The law says that the younger brother "goes in to her." Some argue that the duty of the younger brother is simply to have sexual relations with the woman however many times it takes to produce a child. They limit his obligation to reproduction. After he produces an heir, she returns to widowhood, and he returns to his former ways. This may have been common in pagan cultures, but the Bible indicates that this union is consummated as a marriage. Given the legal obligation, the sexual union or consummation is all that is needed to initiate the levirate marriage. Here we see that as the younger brother has union with the woman, he consummates his relationship as a *true marriage*.

Granted, there is not a lot of fanfare or romance associated with this approach, but consummation seems to be the primary action that initiates or enacts the marriage. This explains why Ruth simply approaches Boaz to cover her, or to have sexual relations with her, and in so doing he would have initiated the levirate marriage. This all comes together to indicate that the younger brother who is acting as a redeemer takes the woman as a true wife and not just for producing offspring. As redeemer-husband he is obligated to care for her and love her. This is not just a sexual arrangement for producing male babies.

Bigamy?

It is not entirely clear if this practice allowed for having two wives, bigamy, but it seems, rather, to exclude it. In other words, what would be the obligation of the younger brother if he is already married? Does he still have to maintain his duty as a levir? Since the law in its context points to the younger brother who remains in his father's house, this younger brother is almost certainly single. It is reasonable to assume that if this younger brother were outside the house, then he would be married and no longer in line for this duty. Furthermore, Leviticus 18:18 forbids a man from marrying his wife's sister. This would seem to forbid a man from taking his brother's wife if he is already married, in that his brother's wife would be his wife's sister. This text in general discouraged taking a second wife. However, the levirate law is an exception in so many ways that we can't be sure. We do know that God's laws never encouraged bigamy or polygamy in any other ways. Therefore it is very doubtful that the younger brother would be obliged to keep this law if he were already married—making this an extreme exception. As noted, the younger brother's place in his father's house implies that he is single. There is difficulty in understanding certain aspects of such laws, and since God hasn't given us a great number of details, we could conclude that he wants us to focus on the principles more than the details.

Genesis 38

From start to finish in Ruth, the levirate laws provide the needed remedy for our widows. They not only provide the remedy for the immediate and particular problem of Elimelech's death, but they also provide a more powerful remedy for the family of David more broadly. In fact, the rather uncomfortable story of incest in Genesis 38 provoked the crisis we have in the story of Ruth. These two stories are connected in many important ways.

In Genesis 38 we learn that Judah had three sons named Er, Onan, and Shelah. Judah's firstborn son was the covenant representative for the family. However, he died.

Following the levirate laws, Judah gave his next son, Onan, to his daughter-in-law, Tamar. Like his older brother, Onan angered the Lord, and God killed him.

There are many strange commentaries that have attempted to use Onan's sins as an example of how God hates birth control. Some argue that this story proves God's disapproval of other related sexual activities. This is simply not the case. We are not forbidden to exercise godly dominion over reproduction any more than we are forbidden to exercise godly dominion in every other area of our lives.

Onan's sin was not birth control but a stubborn, selfish refusal to fulfill his obligations to his older brother—and thus to God. Moses teaches us that Onan rejected God and was in essence attempting to steal the inheritance for himself. Onan sought to steal the inheritance and refused to produce a son who would take his brother's name and receive the inheritance. When we interpret this passage, we must use the levirate laws as the context and not our own personal views on birth control. Context always governs our interpretation of Scripture.

The Reason for the Law

Deuteronomy states explicitly that the purpose for this law was that the name of the deceased man may not be blotted out of Israel, to preserve the name of the deceased brother in the land. According to Deuteronomy 25:6, the firstborn son of the levirate arrangement took the name and all the inheritance of the deceased older brother. This means that the arrangements provided by the law were not focused on the land alone as a part of the inheritance but on the name as well. While it is true that the firstborn son inherited the land portion, this was not the complete focus of the levirate law.

Preserving the name is the focus of the levirate law. The

story in Genesis 38 also reminds us that God's people were to keep the levirate law even before the land was given to Israel. This indicates that the obligations in the levirate laws most likely pre-dated the land portions of the Torah.

The Name

The land was given as a stewardship for the families. The family name was attached to the land, and thus it was important because it related to this stewardship. In the Bible a name refers to the total person, the whole of someone is theologically, and it has far-reaching implications in Old Testament literature. This is why we are told to pray in Jesus' name. We pray to him and all that he is as our Lord and Savior.

When we are baptized, we are baptized into his name. We are, as such, placed in union with the name of our God— Father, Son, and Holy Spirit: "But as many as received Him, to them He gave the right to become children of God, to those who believe in His *name*" (John 1:12).

In the Old Covenant, all that a person was and all that he had was summed up in the name; it was everything. This is not the case today in the New Covenant. We are not concerned about names in the same way that our forefathers in the Old Testament were concerned. This is one specific way Jesus has changed things for us.

For instance, I have great hope for my sons. I pray that they will carry on my family name with honor. But there is a radical difference between my hope for a good reputation and the Old Testament longing to give birth to Messiah. We are no longer hoping for Messiah to come from our own families. Consequently, we don't tend to name our children in the same way as our Old Testament forebears. Recently I baptized Winston Christopher Emerson. I love that name. It reminds me, of course, of one of my favorite historical figures, Winston Churchill. It also has a rather aristocratic ring to it. It sounds noble. However, his name is not the name in which we hope. It is in the name of Jesus that we hope today. We have a new name in Jesus.

My father and I talked recently about our namesakes. My dad's name is Lloyd Charles Jackson; I am Lloyd Charles Jackson Jr.; and my son is Lloyd Charles Jackson, III. We jokingly hope that all the problems associated with our family will get better with each generation. Perhaps there will be some kind of a growth in purity. However, as Christians, we do not ultimately hope in our family's name but only in the name of Jesus. Do you see how the preservation of the Old Testament names was pointing to the name of our Savior Jesus?

Levir and Kinsman-Redeemer

Since the family's name was so important, what would happen if all the sons died, as in Ruth's story? What happens to a family when there is no younger brother? What does the family do when there aren't any more sons? As I mentioned earlier, the responsibilities extended outwardly to the father's brother's family. In other words, cousins apparently had a voluntary responsibility to stand in the place of the younger brother. This is what happened in the story of Ruth. Incidentally (or not so incidentally), this family member who stood in the place of the younger brother was called the redeemer. We often see the word translated *kinsman-redeemer*.

The Redeemer or *Goel*

You can begin to see how the levirate laws are important in the book of Ruth. In Ruth 2:20, Naomi states that Boaz is a redeemer, recognizing that Boaz is a redeemer for the household. The redeemer had a few standard duties in the ancient world. Perhaps the most important one charged him with the responsibility to seek justice in the case of a family member's death. If a family member were murdered, then the redeemer was charged with tracking the murderer and bringing him to justice. If the murderer had not sought refuge in the cities of refuge, then the redeemer was to kill the murderer. In fact, his job was to chase the murderer and avenge the death before the murderer could reach the city of refuge. This was one of the central duties of the *goel,* or kinsman-redeemer. Naomi says that this man Boaz is our *goel,* avenger of blood, redeemer.

The *goel* was also the one who was responsible to buy a person back who had been sold into slavery. If a person were forced to sell his land, it would be the *goel's* job as the redeemer to buy back the land. The redeemer, then, was the man who took the place of one who was unable to fulfill his covenant responsibility. He was the one who legally performed for another that which he was unable to do for himself. A person's inability could be due to slavery, debt, or perhaps—as is the case in our story—death. The redeemer fulfilled other family responsibilities, such as acting as a levirate husband.

The *goel,* or redeemer, had the responsibility to care for justice and righteousness for his family. His job was to make things right on behalf of his family. As we delve deeper into the meaning of the kinsman-redeemer, we not only gain deep insight into Boaz and his actions but we will also ascertain something of the richness of Christ's redemption and love for his people.

Typology

All of these seemingly strange and uncomfortable laws and arrangements are difficult to reconcile with our present social and cultural norms. Yet they begin to make sense when we read them with Christ and his covenant promises in view. One of the reasons we have so many problems understanding is that we fail to put the whole Bible together as one book. One of the many ways we see the Old and New Testaments fitting together is through *typology.* Typology is when Old Testament persons or events point forward. They are sometimes called shadows of the future. These types or patterns of things to come often lead straight to Jesus. Understanding this not only helps us to make sense of some of the Old Testament teachings but also actually brings them to life for us. As we come to understand the Old Testament, it becomes a beautiful and inspiring part of our lives.

When we read the Old Testament, we can and should ask some interesting theological questions regarding types. For instance, was there ever an older brother who represented the whole of humanity in the Bible? The answer is yes; his name was Adam. He was the older brother. Adam was the covenant head or federal representative. Adam was the older brother who refused to do his job. He fell from the estate wherein he was created by sinning against God. Consequently, he died: "He was cut off from the future by death. In Adam and in his name there was no hope of any future for his descendants."[1]

Because of the fall into sin, all of Adam's descendants were cursed and unable to fulfill their calling. None of Adam's descendants was able to fulfill the cultural mandate. This mandate included the idea of living with a sense of purpose towards the future—being fruitful and multiplying. Adam was supposed to fill the earth and to subdue it. When he sinned, he died, and therefore he could not fulfill his purpose; in Adam all hope was lost.

God had promised Adam that the future hope of salvation would come through his seed. But because of sin, Adam died and couldn't fulfill his task; he could not produce such seed. Without any posterity, no savior would ever be born.

---

1   Jim Jordan, audio series, *Ruth.*

Therefore, someone new, a younger brother, was needed to take his place. A new covenant representative would be needed to fulfill Adam's role as covenant representative— Jesus the Christ.

When you approach the Old Testament in this way, you see immediately that the levirate laws are fulfilled in Christ. The name of the faithful belongs no longer to this or that family but to Jesus. Thus we no longer have the same concerns about our family names and how the land is connected to those names. We have a new name in Christ: we are Christians.

Jesus Christ is the kinsman-redeemer who replaced Adam as the new covenant head of his people. Jesus does for his people what Adam was unable to do for them. God had predestined for his people to be saved, and the fall of Adam was not going to frustrate his will. This theme is woven beautifully into the fabric of the book of Genesis. Indeed, this is true throughout the entire Bible, but especially in Genesis. As a theme it resurfaces, especially in regard to Jacob and Esau. God makes us understand that the older brother will not be the one who saves his people.

> And not only this, but when Rebecca also had conceived by one man, even by our father Isaac (for the children not yet being born, nor having done any good or evil, that the purpose of God according to election might stand, not of works but of Him who calls), it was said to her, "The older shall serve the younger." As it is written, "Jacob I have loved, but Esau I have hated" (Rom. 9:10–13).

Have you ever wondered about the number of Bible stories that focus on the relationships between brothers? Have you also ever wondered why God intervenes in his sovereignty to ensure that we see his sovereign work in salvation in these stories? Not only do these stories teach predestination but they also witness to the older brother's inability to do what another one (a younger brother) will need to do for him.

God reveals that all of man's efforts to gain salvation are impotent; they are dead. Only God provides salvation, and he does so through the younger brother who brings new life. When Adam sinned, he died and was disqualified as the covenant representative; Eve was widowed without any hope for the future. As the younger brother, Christ fulfills what Adam could not do as the older brother. Christ, as the new covenant representative, raised up a seed for Adam. This was in fact the gospel promise made in Genesis 3:15: "And I will put enmity between you and the woman, and between your seed and her Seed; He shall bruise your head, and you shall bruise His heel."

Christians not only fulfill the cultural mandate but they also become partakers with Jesus in the victory over the wicked one. The promise was that the seed of the woman would crush the head of the serpent: "And the God of peace will crush Satan under your feet shortly. The grace of our Lord Jesus Christ be with you. Amen" (Rom. 16:20).

The hope of Messiah who would come through the seed of the woman was maintained in the levirate marriage. Consequently, the levirate laws are no longer relevant to the new covenant. Christ has come, and we are no longer under any of the typological shadows that pointed to his coming.

Christ's name is now the only name that must be maintained. Today Christians are no longer under any obligation to maintain their name. While most people desire to maintain their family line, it is not a religious necessity. Yes, we want our family name to be of good repute. Yet we have no biblical mandate to maintain our own particular name through a male heir.

While we should desire to have a godly reputation for our family, it is also possible to fall into the trap of idolizing our family's name. Some people seek immortality through their children and desire to live forever in the names of their children. This is a common practice with pagans. God has given us a natural desire for eternal life, and pagans pervert this desire as they dream of immortality through their children.

We have no hope for salvation through our own names. In Christ, no death may ever cause our inheritance to die. Because of the resurrection, we have eternal life in the name of Christ. Indeed, our name is Christian. This is the name of our inheritance, and this is the hope for the future. In Christ, we have permanence, and our name will never be blotted out. Christ's name is our name.

If we don't have any children to maintain our inheritance, it no longer matters in a covenantal sense. Christ our Savior is the name into which and by which we are saved. He is the promised seed and the husband. He is the younger brother, the second Adam. As Messiah, Christ is both of these at the same time.

Christ becomes for his church the husband who saves her. The first husband, Adam, died, but in the second Adam, Christ, we are made alive. Christ is the true husband, and in Christ we are called to fulfill what Adam could not fulfill. We now possess the land of Adam, which is the whole earth. The picture of this hope was given partially in the levirate laws. We have it now fulfilled completely in Christ. We depend on Jesus, the younger brother, to do everything for us and for our children that we could never do ourselves.

The levirate laws, like so many of the Old Testament laws, reminded the people that God would provide a redeemer as a means of saving his people, even in the face of death. Salvation would not come through men's own efforts or the efforts of their children; it would be through God alone.

Questions for Consideration
1. What is the origin of the name *levirate?*
2. Give a summary of the levirate laws and where they are found in the Scriptures.
3. What were the duties of the younger brother?
4. What was the primary purpose of this arrangement?
5. Why was God angry at Judah's sons in Genesis 38?
6. What was important about a name in the Bible?
7. What was the role of the kinsman-redeemer, or *goel?*
8. How does the redeemer's role relate to the levirate laws?
9. What are the many ways that Jesus fulfills this role for us?

Lesson 11

The Ultimate Philanthropist

Ruth 4

Perhaps you have heard of a heart-warming story about a family so deeply in debt that the family could never pay its way out. Then out of nowhere a philanthropist comes along, pays the debt, and delivers them in a way that they could have never delivered themselves. There was a very popular show on TV in America called *Extreme Makeover: Home Edition.* The extreme makeover team would get applications from people all over the nation who were in extreme need. Usually the family had experienced some devastating disease, death, or tragedy that had cost them their home and their ability to rebuild it. With tears in everyone's eyes, the extreme home makeover team would move into place, and within seven days, the team would rebuild the house, while the blessed family was off on some exotic vacation. The family returned to find not just that everything old had been torn down and removed but that they had a brand new, beautiful home. This is a great example of philanthropy.

Throughout the whole story of Ruth, we have witnessed Naomi's family brought to utter destruction and hopelessness; the family's needs were too costly for them to pay. What this family needed was a philanthropist! From the start of the story Samuel presents us with pain, sorrow, and death. The death and destruction that grips Ruth's story calls us to hope for someone to do something that would relieve their pain. Our story marks Boaz as a philanthropist who could do what Naomi and Ruth could never have done for themselves.

What is a philanthropist, and what is philanthropy? Philanthropy is a combination of two Greek terms; *philos*—love—and *anthropos*—man. Hence, at its root, philanthropy means the love of man. Philanthropy is generally defined as the voluntary promotion of human welfare at one's own expense. The philanthropist usually has a deep desire to improve the material, social, and spiritual welfare of humanity, especially through charitable activities.

Another word, *altruism*, is sometimes used to describe this kind of activity. Altruistic concern for human welfare and advancement is an outward, not an inward concern. To be altruistic is to be concerned for others. This is manifested by donations of money, property, or work to needy persons, by endowment of institutions of learning and hospitals, or by generosity to other socially useful purposes.

Even more pointedly, a philanthropist is someone who takes of his own resources and gives it to others without an expectation of return. The reason giving to museums, libraries, and hospitals is considered such a good example of philanthropy is related to the reality that these kinds of institutions don't offer any kind of an immediate financial return on one's investment. The investment is almost entirely for the good of someone else.

Athanasius was fond of using the word philanthropy in his theological work. This word seemed to capture the essence of the incarnation of Jesus. Jesus was a lover of mankind. Perhaps the most characteristic element of Jesus' love was that it was completely selfless. His love was a pouring out of himself on behalf of others. Even more astounding was the fact that this love was poured out toward sinners.

Our Savior is the source of all true philanthropy. Thus, when we find stories in the Bible that point us to Jesus, we find stories of philanthropy. Think about this as we watch our story of Ruth and Boaz move toward its conclusion. Boaz is foreshadowing our Savior, and, as such, he illustrates for us true philanthropy. He is the selfless husband, and Ruth is the blessed wife who humbly receives his love. She opens herself to Boaz as an empty widow, and he fills her. She lies at his feet, and he covers her. This is a beautiful picture of Jesus and the church.

Chapter 4 takes us to the conclusion of this story of philanthropy. The story has taken the final turn towards blessing, but we may still be asking, what will happen next. For the closing scene, Samuel takes us to the city gate.

The Gate

This is like the city council or city courthouse; it is the place of life and death. The men sat down for business because the gates of a city were the place where legal transactions took place. It was the place of entrance for those who were admitted into the city. It was also here at the city gate where one might be denied access to the city. The gate is where someone would be sentenced if he were convicted of a crime. People were stoned to death at the city gates. We see the same idea communicated in the New Testament when Jesus says that the gates of hell will not prevail against the church—the gate represents the authority of the city.

Mr. So-and-so

As they gathered at the gate, Boaz called out to a man who remained noticeably unnamed. He was conspicuously anonymous. In a story where the author uses names to teach theological lessons, the irony can sometimes be humorous. This is especially the case when the reader learns that this nameless relative was afraid of jeopardizing his name. Samuel uses a phrase that has baffled many scholars. Its origin and use is not known. It may have contained a word play, but we can't be certain. Still, almost all agree that it was some kind of a colloquial phrase that could be translated as "so and so." We could humorously call him "Mr. So-and-so." He is deliberately nameless.

Here the nameless character is known to us only as a man who refused to act as redeemer in order to preserve his name. What an irony! The man said essentially, "I can't do this because I will jeopardize my name, my inheritance!" He desperately wanted to do everything he could do to preserve his name, and in so doing, he lost the opportunity to have his name preserved.

It ought to strike us as highly ironic that the man so anxious to preserve his name and his inheritance is not known to us by name. If he would have responded to the duty of the Lord, we would now be speaking of him instead of Boaz. Is this not the paradox of which our Savior spoke in his own ministry? The man who seeks his life will lose it, but he who loses his life for Christ's sake will gain it.

The relative in the story is called upon to serve his distant family member. As the story unfolds, Mr. So-and-so discovers that there won't be any return on his investment in a financial sense. His return would have had to come in being satisfied with helping the relative—in being a servant to a needy family. This is not a return in the common sense of the term. The whole venture involved the very real possibility of investing everything he possessed, only to enhance someone else's estate. Mr. So-and-so did not hold the land in trust because he felt the risk was too great. He wanted the land all for himself or he did not want to have it at all. Hence, he gave Boaz the right to redeem the land and to take Ruth as his wife.

The Catch

At first it looked like purchasing the land would be a great benefit. Mr. So-and-so could have worked it, and he could potentially have reaped all the rewards. However, there was

a huge catch—redeeming the land also required him to be
a redeemer for Ruth. Notice that Boaz purposefully waited
to reveal this to Mr. So-and-so. Boaz deliberately linked the
land together with the levirate laws. The transaction and
our whole story involved far more than a piece of land—
this was about performing the duty of a younger brother
as outlined in Deuteronomy 25. Hence, Boaz wanted to
draw this man into a public rejection of his duties so as to
seal the whole deal with witnesses in a court of law. There
would be no doubt about who was Ruth's true husband
because of the way the man actually removed himself from
the scene with his own words.

Notice how Boaz drew Mr. So-and-So into renouncing
his claims with a kind of "Oh, by the way" statement. This
piece of land needed to be purchased in order to keep the
land in the family—the extended family. You will notice
that Boaz didn't mention Ruth at first. Rather, he spoke
only of the land. "Then Boaz said, 'On the day you buy the
field from the hand of Naomi, you must also buy it from
Ruth the Moabitess, the wife of the dead, to perpetuate the
name of the dead through his inheritance.' And the close
relative said, 'I cannot redeem it for myself, lest I ruin my
own inheritance. You redeem my right of redemption for
yourself, for I cannot redeem it'" (vv. 5–6).

If Ruth had one son by this man, the boy would have had
Elimelech's name, and he could possibly have gained this
man's inheritance if he had no more sons. Remember, the
levirate laws require the firstborn son to belong to the older
brother. This seems to imply that the rest of the children
born to this family would belong to the younger brother.
Hence, humanly speaking, it was a bit of a gamble. This
might have involved a huge investment, and it could have
cost him in many ways. Likewise, there was a very real
possibility of little and even no return for this man. There
was always a calculated risk in every investment. This man

simply thought that the risks outweighed the costs at this time. After all, his entire investment might be lost in one sense.

At this the man decided not to purchase the land. If he bought the land, he would not get to keep it or pass it on to his own sons. Rather, he would purchase the land only to hold it in trust for the firstborn of the dead man. Any sons that he may have who would bear his name would not get the investment of the land. The firstborn son would bear the name of Elimelech, and the land would belong to Elimelech's son. Consequently, this man's firstborn son could possibly inherit the land, in which he was now making an investment. Perhaps the risk was fine if he were assured of a long-term return. Yet, with the very real possibility that this man might lose the land quickly, he reconsidered his investment. What if he had only one son? Then not only this piece of land but all of the rest of his inheritance might have gone to Elimelech's heirs.

The Hebrew language indicates that Ruth actually owned the land and was going to sell it. If it were just the land, then the man could have had the property all to himself. Perhaps he could have sold it at a profit. Maybe he saw this as a sheriff's sale, and he was hoping to turn it around quickly. More than likely he could have purchased the land, developed it, and added it to his whole estate, and then he could have passed it on to his children as part of his inheritance at least until the Year of Jubilee. God had given the various laws regarding the land not so his people could keep it forever. Rather, God tested the faithful—would they grasp after an inheritance of their own making, or would they trust in the Lord and give it back freely to the previous family?

It could have been that Naomi had rights to a portion of a common field in which many families shared. This would have made it very difficult for her to obtain it as a widow.

It would also have made this man's purchase a sweet deal. He could have increased his investment, and he would have experienced an immediate return on the land at the next harvest. Samuel doesn't record the exact details, but at least from Mr. So-and-so's perspective, he thought he could make a one-time transaction and profit from the land. But there was a catch, and her name was Ruth.

I Cannot Redeem:

Boaz brilliantly maneuvered Mr. So-and-so into making the public proclamation, "I cannot redeem." In saying this he removed himself from the scene. His words reflect the symbolic exchange of the sandal that takes place later. He was ready and willing to take the land when it was only the land, but when Boaz connected all the dots of his responsibility, he stepped aside willingly.

This man's response was a classically selfish response. He was not acting in selfless faith to the duty of the Lord. Like Elimelech, he was faithless. His actions remind us of Onan, in Genesis 38, who refused to perform the duty of the levirate for Tamar. These are the kinds of men who preferred a piece of land to the will of God. He was selfish and confused, grasping after something that would never preserve his name, and in so doing he removed himself from our story. Ironically Mr. So-and-so disappears forever as a nameless failure.

The Sandal

When Mr. So-and-so refused to carry out his duty, he was required to show this publicly by exchanging his sandals. Why a sandal, and what does this mean? As noted in the previous chapter, Ruth provides evidence of the levirate laws in action. We find some help from Deuteronomy 25:7–10.

But if the man does not want to take his brother's wife,

then let his brother's wife go up to the gate to the elders, and say, "My husband's brother refuses to raise up a name to his brother in Israel; he will not perform the duty of my husband's brother." Then the elders of his city shall call him and speak to him. But if he stands firm and says, "I do not want to take her," then his brother's wife shall come to him in the presence of the elders, remove his sandal from his foot, spit in his face, and answer and say, "So shall it be done to the man who will not build up his brother's house." And his name shall be called in Israel, "The house of him who had his sandal removed."

Spits in His Face
The reader notices that Ruth's story does not include the infamous "spitting in the face." This is quite obviously an expression of contempt and shame. One need not possess great insight into the nuances of the Hebrew language— it is safe to say that spitting in someone's face is a fairly universal action of scorn. Samuel conspicuously leaves this out of the sandal exchange in Ruth's story.

Ruth's story also omits the woman's removing of the man's sandal, which was used as a symbolic action of shame. Because the man in Deuteronomy 25 refused to raise up seed for his dead brother, he was publicly humiliated as impotent. He was shamed as one who is unable to perform his duty as a levirate. It also indicated that this man refused to stand in his own shoes in regard to this responsibility. He deserved to be ashamed because he refused to maintain his obligations.

In Deuteronomy 25, the widow pulls off the man's sandal, spits in his face, and declares his disgrace using a new name. Now most of us today don't think of the name, "the one whose sandal is removed" as a blight on our reputation. It may sound a bit odd, but it doesn't seem to carry the kind of intense humiliation that this procedure must have carried in ancient Israel. However, we should note that this was something very significant. "Now this was the custom in former times in Israel concerning redeeming and exchanging, to confirm anything: one man took off his sandal and gave it to the other, and this was a confirmation in Israel" (Ruth 4:7).

What Samuel recorded in Ruth's story is not this kind of shame, but it does involve something similar. In our scene we should notice that there was no shame in the transaction, since neither one of these men was the younger brother. Hence, the handing of the sandal seemed to indicate that one man was transferring his obligations or responsibilities to another. It was as if to say, "You walk in my sandals in this matter." The issue did not involve public shame connected to levirate refusal as in Deuteronomy 25, but it represented the idea of a transfer of duty and responsibility.

> And Boaz said to the elders and all the people, "You are witnesses this day that I have bought all that was Elimelech's, and all that was Chilion's and Mahlon's, from the hand of Naomi. Moreover, Ruth the Moabitess, the widow of Mahlon, I have acquired as my wife, to perpetuate the name of the dead through his inheritance, that the name of the dead may not be cut off from among his brethren and from his position at the gate. You are witnesses this day" (Ruth 4:9–10).

Boaz showed himself to be the responsible man. He stepped into the shoes of the kinsman-redeemer and carried out his duty. Likewise, Boaz became the mediator between the deaths of the early part of our story and the life that is to come at the end. Boaz opened the future to resurrection life.

Resurrection
As Ruth's story concludes, perhaps the clearest theme of all is the idea of resurrection from the dead. In this final

transaction we see the dead raised to life. The names of the two deceased brothers were mentioned in reverse order from the earlier portion of the story. Samuel may have done this to remind us that Boaz's actions reversed their deaths, and that through Boaz, God would bring new life to the family.

Boaz is the *goel*—remember that *goel* is the Hebrew word for kinsman-redeemer. This was the family member charged with the responsibility of caring for the welfare of the family, even at his own expense. The redeemer would buy back land, pay debts, and set prisoners free. He would stand in the place of the helpless, or in this case, in the place of the dead. He stood for those who could not stand for themselves. The redeemer stood in the place of the widow and the orphan. The redeemer stood in the place of the helpless man who had fled to a city of refuge under the threat of death. The redeemer was the ultimate philanthropist, because his actions did not directly benefit him. The whole concept demanded a selfless love for others.

In Ruth's story the redeemer was a lawyer—Boaz was the resurrection lawyer. The concept of *goel* involved the idea of prosecuting justice on behalf of someone who had no legal standing. He played the messianic roles of our Savior in so many ways. For example, Boaz stood as an advocate in a court case. Remember that the gate of the city was the ancient courthouse. Thus, Boaz was prosecuting justice on behalf of Naomi and Ruth. Boaz would not allow the first relative to take advantage of Ruth or Naomi. He stood as the advocate for these two helpless widows. In Ruth's story, Boaz rightly combined the concepts of redemption and the levirate laws. Because Boaz stood in the gap, Mr. Selfish So-and-so was not allowed to take the land and run away from his responsibilities.

When the unnamed relative agreed to one part of his obligation, Boaz pressed the claims of Ruth according to the levirate laws. Whoever stood in the place of the redeemer also had marriage obligations that came with the land. He had to be a true husband who was concerned for his family and the land. Samuel presented redemption as a powerful concept when it was melded together with the obligations of a redeemer and a husband.

Boaz advocated justice for Naomi as a widow with no apparent base of support from her family, because they had all died. Boaz also stood as the advocate for Ruth, a widow and a foreigner, who was in an even more precarious position. Boaz stood where these two women could not have stood on their own—he was their advocate.

Resurrection and new life propels us forward into the resurrection chain of blessings, which leads us directly to our Savior, Jesus. Indeed, our standing before God is commonly linked to a courtroom and throne scene. The judge looms over us as we are helpless, but God provides an advocate. Notice 1 John 1:9–10, "If we confess our sins, He is faithful and just to forgive us our sins and to cleanse us from all unrighteousness. If we say that we have not sinned, we make Him a liar, and His word is not in us." Also, notice these words, "My little children, these things I write to you, so that you may not sin. And if anyone sins, we have an Advocate with the Father, Jesus Christ the righteous. And He Himself is the propitiation for our sins, and not for ours only but also for the whole world" (1 John 2:1–2).

It is Jesus who pleads our cause and lifts us from our knees as we are under condemnation to a position where we he provides us mercy and justice. He takes us as his own. He gives himself as our mediator and husband. We are his bride. The whole of the story of Ruth drives us forward to the story of Jesus. Yes, as we have said repeatedly, Ruth's story is our story.

Bible Studies on Ruth

Jesus, the Ultimate Philanthropist

What Jesus does as our advocate cost him dearly. Indeed, our Savior gave everything with nothing to gain. Love from Jesus flows outward like the images of the rivers of water that flow from the temple in Ezekiel 47. He was punished so we would not be. He was lashed and beaten so we could avoid the beating we so rightly deserve. Oh Christian, do you appreciate his philanthropy? Jesus has given more than any millionaire has ever given to the cause of libraries, schools, or hospitals. He sacrificed himself for us, and it cost him everything.

Jesus was scourged and beaten, mocked and hated, but why? What did he do to deserve such scorn? What did he do to deserve the betrayal and the hatred? What did he do to deserve the crown of thorns or the nails that pierced his hands and feet? He gave himself entirely on behalf of sinners—he is the ultimate philanthropist. Listen to the well-known but never too familiar prophecy of God's philanthropy, of God's love for sinners in Isaiah 53:4–8,

> Surely He has borne our griefs and carried our sorrows; yet we esteemed Him stricken, smitten by God, and afflicted. But He was wounded for our transgressions, He was bruised for our iniquities; the chastisement for our peace was upon Him, and by His stripes we are healed. All we like sheep have gone astray; we have turned, every one, to his own way; and the LORD has laid on Him the iniquity of us all. He was oppressed and He was afflicted, Yet He opened not His mouth; He was led as a lamb to the slaughter, and as a sheep before its shearers is silent, so He opened not His mouth. He was taken from prison and from judgment, and who will declare His generation? For He was cut off from the land of the living; for the transgressions of My people He was stricken.

What a contrast! We see the selfish, unnamed relative evanescing into the vaporous halls of history's unknown.

The selfish man who struggles and strives to protect his name is never named and disappears forever. Only the philanthropist remains! Only the one who gives his life to God and neighbor will have an eternal inheritance. He through Christ will have an everlasting name.

Where are you in this story? Are you struggling desperately to preserve what can't be preserved by your own efforts? Or will you be like Ruth, who longed to be covered by Boaz? If you will come to Christ, as Ruth came to Boaz, then you will encounter the ultimate philanthropist, and you will find the ultimate love!

Questions for Consideration

1. What is philanthropy? Can you give some examples?
2. What is the significance of the city gate?
3. What is the significance of the name, "Mr. So-and-so?"
4. Why does Ruth's story omit the spitting of Deuteronomy 25?
5. Why do Boaz and Mr. So-and-so exchange sandals?
6. How was Boaz an advocate, and how is this like Jesus?
7. Do you agree that Jesus was the ultimate philanthropist? Explain.

A Genealogy of Grace and Hope for the Future

The story of Ruth concludes with a genealogy—but why? "Why end this beautiful story with a family tree, a piece of dusty historical information about long-dead people?"[1] Samuel moves us from famine to harvest, from faithlessness to faithfulness, from widowhood to marriage, from barrenness to fruitfulness, and ultimately from death to life. In this sense a birth and a genealogy is a fitting way to conclude Ruth's story. Samuel concludes with resurrection reversal in a genealogy of the child Obed, who will be a "restorer of life." Obed's birth has an unmistakable connection to the future kingdom of David, and thus it drives us into the future. It is not an exaggeration to say that the future course of history was altered with the resurrection/birth at the end of Ruth's story. One scholar notes,

> This short genealogy quickly advances the story's time frame from "long ago" (i.e., "the judges' days") to "recently" (i.e. a time closer to the audience) . . . Suddenly, the simple, clever human story of two struggling widows takes on a startling new dimension. It becomes a bright, radiant thread woven into the fabric of Israel's larger national history . . . Yahweh' guidance takes on new meaning. His gracious care for two defenseless widows now emerges as divine guidance

---

1   Ferguson, *Faithful God*, 144.

for the benefit of all Israel.[2]

The genealogy authenticates the kingdom of David, pushing the promises of David's kingdom far into the future. Think of it—David's kingdom was historically connected with resurrection as the means by which it was established and as the means by which it would move into the future. Thus the kingdom of David was a kingdom of resurrection life. LaCocque says, "The whole book of Ruth is also centered on the perpetuation of the generations in Israel, and by extension, on the indispensable culmination of salvation history—here in the person of David, then in the Messiah."[3]

Therefore, the concluding genealogy has redemptive / theological dimensions that are *eschatological*. This is a fancy way of saying that Samuel uses this story to point us forward into history toward the last things—the culmination of history itself in the coming of Messiah's kingdom. Imagine—all of that from a genealogy!

The Theology of Genealogy

Genealogies played an important role in Jewish culture. In fact they were so important that Paul gave specific warning against the misuse of genealogies. It may strike contemporary readers as rather odd that of all the things Paul could have warned the people of God to avoid, he told them to avoid disputes over genealogies. He says, in 1 Timothy 1:4, "nor give heed to fables or endless genealogies, which cause disputes rather than godly edification which is in faith."

The Hebrew people were acutely aware of the importance of history, and they used genealogies to link themselves to

---

2   Ron L. Hubbard Jr., *The Book of Ruth* (Grand Rapids: Eerdmans, 1988), 277–278.

3   André LaCocque, *Ruth*, 118.

the past. They were the people of God, and this could be traced through their genealogies. Genealogies are sprinkled almost everywhere across the pages of the Old Testament. Rarely is a person mentioned in the Old Testament without at least some brief reference to his or her genealogical roots. (Joshua, son of Nun; Solomon, son of David.) While many of us skip or ignore biblical genealogies, genealogies were very important to the people of God. But why? Why did God use genealogies in the Bible? Was this merely for the sake of establishing a good pedigree? There were many practical reasons for emphasizing genealogies.

Land

A family's place of residence in the land was determined by tribes, families, and father's houses (Num. 26:52–56; 33:54), Sometimes, in order to establish one's claim to property, it was legally necessary to produce a valid genealogy to substantiate one's claim. The transfer of land required accurate knowledge of genealogy (Ruth 3:9, 12–13; 4:1–10).

Employment

In order to lay claim to certain jobs in the religious system that was central to Israel, one had to produce a valid genealogy. For instance, to become a member of the most important social class among the Jewish people, the priesthood, one had to produce a genealogy connecting him to the family of Aaron. Upon return from Babylon a person claiming priestly prerogatives was required to provide a genealogy proving priestly descent (Ezra 2:62). Genealogies were especially important for the high priestly job. Jobs in the temple also were connected to the tribe of Levi.

Title

Anyone claiming a title of leadership had to produce genealogical evidence for the claim. Indeed, royal succession

was linked with Davidic lineage (1 Kings 11:36; 15:4).
Genealogies played a very practical role in the social /
political life of the Hebrew people. The genealogy with
which Matthew begins his gospel is not an attempt to claim
a high pedigree for Jesus. Rather, its principal intention is
to substantiate Jesus' claim to a title, the claim to the
title *Christ*.

Genealogies Link Us to the Past for a Sense of the Future
The practical reasons were connected with the theological
reasons. Genealogies link us to the past as something
vital for our future. This may be hard for many of us to
appreciate as modern / post-modern thinkers. We tend to
have a distrust of things that are old. We tend to deride
and to disdain the aged and the ancient. Consequently,
we don't have a great deal of interest in history, historical
things, or—least of all—genealogies. In fact, for some
of us, genealogies may well be the lowest on the scale of
historically interesting things to study.

The Bible is structured to oppose this way of thinking.
It may also help to remember that the Bible is a historical
document. The Bible constantly tutors us to appreciate
history. The Bible draws our minds to the redemptive events
of God in history, and from these objective events we are
encouraged to look forward. Genealogies are critical to this
way of thinking. Genealogies link us to the past and provide
us with the memory God wants us to have.

Genealogies don't win beauty prizes for their glamour,
but they are important links in the chain of redemptive
history. There is very little about genealogies that is thrilling
or nostalgic, which seems to be the way God wants them.
As an emotional reflection on the past, God doesn't
encourage nostalgia. We could define nostalgia as a wistful
or excessively sentimental longing to return to some past
period that in reality cannot be recovered. In this sense,

nostalgia is not helpful for Christians. "Nostalgia," says, historian Christopher Lasch, "does not entail the exercise of memory at all, since the past it idealizes stands outside time, frozen in unchanging perfection." Memory, on the other hand, "draws hope and comfort from the past in order to enrich the present."[4] Biblical genealogies do exactly this—they require us to build on the past, and as such they not only enrich our present but they also inspire us into the future.

Family History?
We generally use genealogies to help us trace our family history. Do you know your family history? I enlisted the help of a local genealogical expert to help me in discovering more about my family's history on the Jackson side. I might add that, unless you are willing to be honest about your "roots," this can be a dangerous endeavor. Genealogies are a double-edged sword. The danger comes, of course, if you are not prepared to discover connections that you didn't really want to unearth. For instance, I tried to persuade my genealogist to find some kind of genealogical connection to Stonewall Jackson. If not Stonewall, then I hoped she might at least connect me to Andrew Jackson or perhaps some noble hero of American history or maybe a distant relative who was instrumental in the Protestant Reformation. Instead, she told me that there were a lot more Irish Catholics in my family than I was willing to admit. For a long time my wife's Irish Catholic connections had been the brunt of family jokes. Now my wife happily redirects the same old jokes back to my side of the family.

Genealogies link us back not only to the good portions but to everything. The good, the bad, and the ugly are all

4   Christopher Lasch, *The True and Only Heaven: Progress and Its Critics* (New York: Norton, 1991), 82ff. I am indebted for this quote to John Muether, historian for the Orthodox Presbyterian Church.

part of who we are in our family history. If genealogies are studied properly, they provide a true sense of "rootedness." If you study your family's history through genealogies, you may find yourself amused. In so many cases, those of us who know our family history find ourselves amused and comforted when we say, for example, "Well this is definitely the 'Jackson' coming out in that boy."

Knowing your family history can inspire you to continue to be faithful. I am proud of my father, for instance, because he broke a long chain in his immediate family history. Neither of his parents finished high school, and he was the first member of his family to go to college. He not only went to college but he also entered and finished dental school, becoming the first professional in our family. You don't appreciate these kinds of things as a child, but the older you get, the more you appreciate your family history and the way such history can be beneficial in so many ways.

Knowing your family's genealogy can give you a sense of steadiness and hope. You can think back about what God has done through your ancestors, and you find courage and hope for what God may do through you. Very few of us have this sense of history rooted in our own experience—a few of you may. We are close friends with a family in Ohio that has a sign at the entrance of their farm reading, "Keys homestead—established 1836." This means that the present Keys family who live on this farm can trace their heritage on the land for several generations. Needless to say, when Dad Keys passed away and the funeral procession slowed down as it passed the Keys farm, the deep family connections to their farm provoked a flood of emotions. In this way a family history can offer a sense of steadiness as we reflect on what God has done in our families in the past. It confirms the basic truth that says, "Knowing where you came from is very helpful in giving you a sense of where you are going in the future."

The Covenant of Grace

Genealogies comprise our family histories; they also structure much of the Bible. The biblical genealogies correspond to the history of redemption—to the covenant of grace. In fact, there is a sense in which the entire Bible is the story of God's covenantal dealings with his people. After the fall, Adam and Eve were hopeless and helpless. God came to them and established a covenant of grace with them (Gen. 3:15). This was the promise of the Messiah who was to come. This covenant of promise was continued through Noah (Gen. 6–9). God was faithful and continued to unfold his covenant of grace with his people as he called out Abraham (Gen. 12, 15, 17).

This covenant of grace always spoke of the same thing: salvation by grace through faith in the Christ. However, the covenant of grace was progressively unfolded to the people of God. They were given a family heritage and a land in which to live. While these promises pointed to specific items (i.e., land), they always pointed beyond themselves to the Christ to come. The land was not to be the permanent dwelling of the people; rather the whole earth—indeed, a new heaven and a new earth—was the future promise.

Please note that there was always a future hope. The items given to Israel were never considered the permanent fulfillment of the covenant of grace. There was always a pointing to the future hope of a Messiah. As the people became a nation with specific laws for morality and for worship, God unfolded his covenant to them even more. He made what some call the covenant of the kingdom (2 Sam. 7). Finally, in Jeremiah 31 we have a promise of a new covenant, the final covenant in this series of covenants, all comprising the covenant of grace. This points us to the Christ, and we should see the connected and intimately interwoven nature of the covenant of grace. It was not their culture, their race, or their land that gave the people of God their identity; the people of God were always saved by grace through faith in the Christ—this was their identity.

The Covenant of Grace Unfolds and Remains Connected
Matthew began his gospel with the words *biblios geneseos,* a book of genealogy or a book of beginnings. The genealogy traces two major lines: the line of Abraham and the line of David. Jesus came as the perfect fulfillment of the covenant promises given to Abraham and David. The New Testament, no less than the Old Testament, includes genealogies. In fact, Matthew began with the same phrase that is used in Genesis 2:4 and 5:1 in the *Septuagint,* the Greek translation of the Hebrew Old Testament.

The entire book of Genesis is structured around the Hebrew word *toledot.* This word, sometimes rendered "the generations of" or "the genealogy of," introduces the new developments in the Genesis narrative (5:1; 6:9; 10:1; 11:10, 27; 25:12, 19; 36:1, 9; 37:2), Genesis is structured according to genealogical / family histories. From the very beginning, God used the structure of the family to define history. The genealogies emerge as the skeletal structure of redemptive history. Adam represented his descendants, and after his fall into sin, the families that issued from him followed different genealogies: Cain's descendants (line of Satan), and Abel's descendants (line of the woman). This idea continues as family genealogies define redemptive history for us. Abel's descendants lead us to Noah. And we all know that Noah and his family entered the ark just before the flood. From the ark the different sons arose and immediately continued the story of how the different generations or genealogies would move into history.

Abraham and his family were called out and continued the story of families in Genesis 12, 15, and 17. Moses was called to lead the descendants of Abraham, and the genealogies became even more defined. In all of these stories, God was honoring covenantal promises. It helps to notice that the promises were never exclusively ethnic. They were comprised of families, but not by pure blood lines. The emphasis on ethnicity was a consistent mistake of the Israelites, a misunderstanding of God's intent.

When Matthew began his gospel with a genealogy, he was offering proof that Jesus was the Christ. Christ was not his name but his title. *Christos* means "the anointed one." Jesus bears the title of the one who is the Messiah. He is Jesus *the Christ*. All of the promises related to the coming Messiah were pointing to the Christ, Jesus. The genealogy is substantive proof of Jesus' claim to this title. The rest of the gospel continues to offer conclusive evidence that Jesus is, indeed, the Christ.

We see Jesus connected to the covenant through Abraham, and we also have evidence of Jesus' connection to the kingdom of God through the line of David. Note 2 Samuel 7:12 and 16: "When your days are fulfilled and you rest with your fathers, I will set up your seed after you, who will come from your body, and I will establish his kingdom forever . . . and your house and your kingdom shall be established forever before you. Your throne shall be established forever."

What Kind of Messiah?
When Jesus arrived in Jerusalem, many Jews expected an ethnic hero to lead them to victory over the Romans—someone to expel the foreigners from the land and establish a Jewish national kingdom. We learn very quickly that God was not concerned with racial purity or spotless ethnic clarity. In fact, it was the genealogy that shattered such a conception of the kingdom of God. God gave the blessings of the genealogies to his sovereign choice so that men would always know that it was not their race or their valiant efforts but the grace of God alone that gained them

salvation; God's sovereign choice, and not man's efforts, is supreme. This is confirmed in Paul's words, "It is not of him who wills nor of him who runs, but of God who shows mercy" (Rom. 9:16). The genealogies teach the sovereignty of God.

- Isaac (from Sarah) not Ishmael
- Jacob and Esau: twins (Gen. 25)
- Perez & Zerah: twins (Gen. 38)
- Joseph (favored though younger)
- Ephraim(younger) and Manasseh (firstborn) (Gen. 48)

This is true of David's kingdom, which was not established by his own strength or his family's efforts. His natural family history included incest and violence. Indeed, he himself was involved in many terrible sins, such as adultery and murder. No, David did not gain his kingdom through his own strength; he gained his kingdom through the resurrection power of God, as Samuel reminds us in Ruth's story.

Don't Be Like the Pharisees!
Be very careful how you think about the kingdom of God. Don't be like the Pharisees, who limited their thinking to a specific ethnic group and a specific plot of ground. When we see the kingdom promises given to God's people as limited to the nation of Israel, we destroy the very nature of the promises as blessing to all the nations of the earth.

Were God's kingdom promises limited to the nation of Israel? Is this period of history in which Ruth lived a parenthesis between the Old Testament kingdom of the past and the Old Testament kingdom of the future? The genealogy in Matthew 1 militates against such a view. Matthew was writing to Jews who apparently had a false understanding of the Messiah to come and who assumed they had ethnic centrality in the covenant promises.

Sometimes having an illustrious genealogy becomes

a source of pride. Perhaps you have read stories of the pride of powerful, aristocratic families who considered themselves elite because of their family history. Certainly this attitude was prevalent among the Jews of Jesus' day. You can virtually hear a proud Jewish father saying, "My family can trace its roots directly back to Abraham himself." "No", said Jesus, "you have misunderstood the purpose of the genealogies. If you think you are something wonderful because you are a descendant of Abraham, you are deceived. "He reminded them that he could make sons of Abraham from stones. The genealogies did not exist to point to ethnic or family pride but to point entirely to the grace and faithfulness of *El Shaddai,* God Almighty.

One of the central purposes of the genealogies was to drive the covenant people away from self-reliance and pride. It was "to show that the reign of David resulted from neither his shrewd politics nor his clever tactics, but from the divine preservation of his worthy family line. Therefore, Israel was to accept David's kingship as the gift of divine guidance."[5]

What fools! Imagine the stupidity of taking pride in that which was supposed to be a source of humility! What audacity the nation had in the days of Jesus! Nothing was supposed to point them to ethnic superiority. God makes this unmistakably clear as he includes the obvious string of foreigners in the genealogies. This should have been conclusive evidence that God's family was not an ethnic family but one of faith.

Incidentally, what a great remedy the church provides for ethnic and racial strife. In the genealogy of grace, God through Christ is gathering all peoples from every tribe and tongue from the earth. The genealogies were never about ethnicity but grace. Certain schools of theology actually

5   Hubbard, *Ruth*, 278.

focus on this mistake—they are obsessed with everything Jewish. They make the same mistake that the Pharisees of Jesus' day made in regard to covenant promises. They assume that God has some sort of ethnic affiliation to the Jews. The family history of Abraham, Isaac, and Jacob was never about ethnicity. Paul makes this very clear in Romans 9, where he states, "Not all who are descended from Israel belong to Israel" (v. 6). It is the faith of families that offers grace to the descendants—not blood or ethnicity. Covenant theology emphasizes this teaching of Scripture; other theologies do not adequately account for this teaching.

A New Family

Jesus Christ came to earth, breaking into the darkness and death of the genealogy of our father Adam. He willingly walked to the cross, taking to Himself the curse and punishment due to all those in the family of Adam and creating for Himself the family of God. Jesus took upon himself the sins of his people. This is why they are faithful; the family of God is faithful because God is faithful. We can't repeat this enough. *The family of God is faithful because God is faithful.* Christians should take personal comfort in this central part of their family history!

Thus the genealogy of grace includes sinners from all the families of the earth. Yes, the genealogies we see in the Bible demand that we notice that the gospel includes the outcasts and the needy. In fact, Jesus' ministry is an amazing account of someone who deliberately went to the outcasts and to the rejected. Jesus blatantly ignored the social, economic, and racial barriers that characterized his day. He included people that nobody else would include. He loved people that nobody else would love. He touched people that nobody else would touch.

The genealogy of grace includes those who willingly submit to the rule of the Lord and who recognize their need of a King—the humble. This means that the genealogy of grace is necessarily going to include people that you and I might naturally have excluded from our family history. For instance, if we were creating our own ideal family history, we might be tempted to leave out crazy Uncle Joey or the cousin who died in prison. Not so the Bible—biblical genealogies are designed to point to God's sovereignty, not to human achievements. This is why so many women and foreigners were included in Christ's genealogy. Note in particular the kind of women in the genealogy.

v. 3—Tamar (Gen. 38)
v. 5—Rahab (the harlot from Jericho)
v. 5—Ruth (Moabitess)
v. 6—Bathsheba (who had been the wife of Uriah the Hittite)

These are the mothers of our faith? Yes, these are the humble women who responded to the call of faith. Not only do these women illustrate the kind of humble saints that God calls to himself but they also highlight for us that this family history is one of grace alone. It may not strike the modern reader as unusual to include women or foreigners, but women and foreigners in particular did not possess the same standing as others did in the ancient world. Contrary to human expectations, the genealogy of grace included women, and not only women but also foreigners and prostitutes. God chooses contrary to human expectations, and his grace is extended to the humble, not the proud.

The Bible is full of all of the stormy conflicts and deceitful conniving that unfaithful men used in an attempt to establish a great family. These schemes or tricks were not only included as a part of the genealogy of the Old Testament, but they seem to constitute the major part of this family history. One theologian noted this well:

> There is undeniably a succession of "improper" events in salvation history . . . To a certain extent, they constitute the

backbone of this history . . . In the name of this (covenantal and eschatological) vision, Jacob is moved by a consuming passion, Rachel demands children or death (Gen. 30:1), and Tamar forces events (Gen. 38). Errors of incalculable proportion are committed: Sarah puts Hagar in Abraham's bed, Lot commits double incest, Jacob "hates" Leah.[6]

Beloved in Christ, the list could go on and on. This is the story of the genealogy of God's family. Think of what LaCocque says: "They constitute the backbone of this history." How did we get where we are? What kept things moving forward? What kept them alive in the midst of all of this sin, deceit, and dysfunction? What propelled them forward as somehow worthy of the attention of God? Stories like Ruth answer the question beyond doubt. Our answer is the sovereign grace of God alone.

Where men strive to grasp after an inheritance, they lose it. Where they deceive in order to gain a name, they are foiled. They lie, cheat, and steal to grasp after what they could never attain by their own efforts. The difference in this family is not their intelligence, their wit, or their wisdom, but the sovereign grace of God. They are, as Paul says in Romans 9, "vessels of grace."

The genealogies do not point us to great men and women as such; they point us to the faithfulness of God. The faithfulness and the grace of God is our family history. Saints of God, you truly have a genealogy of grace! Think of it—in Christ your immediate family history is overpowered and replaced. So many people are hurting and wounded from their immediate family sins, but all who turn to Jesus become members of a new family; they have a genealogy of grace. The faithfulness of God changes our direction and gives us hope.

The biblical genealogies are a tribute to God's faithfulness

---

6   André LaCocque, *Ruth*, 84.

in the face of our sinful unfaithfulness. God is faithful even
when the father of our faith, Abraham, flees to Egypt in
fear. Why did Abraham run to Egypt for help? Quite simply,
Abraham was not always faithful. But God is always
faithful to fulfill his promises. The ultimate faithfulness of
our father Abraham did not come because he possessed an
awesome commitment or a tenaciously courageous spirit; it
emerged because of God's faithfulness to his own covenant
promises.

Biblical authors sometimes used the title *El Shaddai,* God
Almighty, when they wanted to emphasize that God was
faithful in spite of overwhelming odds to the contrary. Yes,
it is *El Shaddai* who provides salvation when men falter and
fail. What a glorious heritage we have in him! This is our
story; this is our genealogy of grace and faithfulness.

We can overcome child abuse, sexual scandals, and a
whole litany of sins that rack our families and our natural
genealogies. We can overcome them because we are now
members of God's family, and God is faithful. Yes, God is
faithful, and the genealogies prove it. We are adopted into
a new genealogy—we are members of a new family who
through Jesus have received the grace of God.

Entering into God's family through Christ shatters the
bonds of slavery that once held us captive as children of our
father Adam. Your father may have been an alcoholic who
beat you and your siblings, but in Christ the genealogy of
sin and darkness is broken. The genealogy of grace shatters
the darkness and bursts the shackles of our former family
ties. The family ties with Adam are not the ties that bind;
it is grace that binds us. Those who become members of
the family of God are in Christ, and they are not bound to
live forever in pornography, greed, or anger. Your father or
mother may have given you birth into a family of death, but
if you turn to the Lord, as Ruth turned to him, then God
gives you new birth into a family of grace and life. It is the

genealogy of Christ that overcomes the genealogy of every sinful family, both now and into the future.

How many people feel overwhelmed by the constraints of family history and thus despair! Some might say, "My dad was an angry, vicious man, and I guess that is all I'll ever be." No, Ruth's story calls you to resurrection power. Ruth's story calls you to Jesus, the husband of a new family. If you turn to Jesus, you are no longer under the dominion of family sins—don't believe any of the "experts" who tell you otherwise.

Our history is hopeful because the genealogies teach us about the faithfulness of God. Don't be convinced of anything else. Do not allow anyone to mislead you about the past. Karl Marx once said that if you deprive a people of their sense of history, you can convince them of anything. This can't be the case with Christians. We have a genealogy of grace that determines our future, and as I have already said, knowing where you came from is very helpful in giving you a sense of where you are going.

This means that your destiny is resurrection living. What an appropriate way to conclude this story of Ruth. Moab was the land of famine and death. If Ruth's destiny belonged to her land, to her people, or to her family, she was born into slavery and death, and thus she had no future. But praise be to the Lord, by his grace Ruth become the mother of Obed in the land of Judah in the city of Bethlehem. God gave her new birth into a new family full of life and hope. Beloved, be encouraged to know that Ruth's story is also our story in the greater Boaz, the greater Obed, even Jesus Christ, our faithful husband.

Questions for Consideration

1. How does a genealogy "advance the time frame" of our story?
2. What does it mean to say Ruth's genealogy is eschatological?
3. What are some reasons people don't like genealogies?
4. How can nostalgia be dangerous?
5. What were three practical reasons Israelites needed genealogies?
6. How are genealogies a double-edged sword?
7. How do genealogies structure the Bible?
8. How do the biblical genealogies teach the sovereignty of God?
9. Why are outcasts, misfits, and "improper" people included in the genealogies?
10. Recount the ways in which the Christian's genealogy of grace encourages us to be faithful.

Note to the Reader

The publisher invites you to respond to us about this book by writing Reformed Fellowship, Inc., 3500 Danube Dr SW, Grandville, MI 49418-8387 USA. You may also email us at *president@reformedfellowship.net*

Founded in 1951, Reformed Fellowship is a religious and strictly nonprofit organization composed of a group of Christian believers who hold to the biblical Reformed faith. Our purpose is to advocate and propagate this faith, to nurture those who seek to live in obedience to it, to give sharpened expression to it, to stimulate the doctrinal sensitivities of those who profess it, to promote the spiritual welfare and purity of the Reformed churches, and to encourage Christian action.

Members of Reformed Fellowship express their adherence to the Calvinistic creeds as formulated in the Belgic Confession, the Heidelberg Catechism, the Canons of Dort, and the Westminster Confession and Catechisms.

To fulfill our mission, we publish a bi-monthly journal, *The Outlook,* and we publish books and Bible study guides. Our website is *www.reformedfellowship.net*